WHY

FISH

CARP?

ACKNOWLEDGEMENTS

In a world of fishes it takes many talented individuals and their contributions to compose the fabric of any piece of literature. It is no different with this book.

With Ol' Puckerpuss's image in our modern outdoors world, it was hard to get many of you to admit to the fact you enjoyed fishing for Mr. Carp. When confronted, many would make claim . . . "I'm just getting them out of the lake" or "I'm bottom feeding for bass and these dam carp just wont stop robbing my bait" and so-on and so-on and so-on. But, every once in a while an old timer would contribute his knowledge or a youngster would show their pride and astonishment or, like the case of my good friend Freddie Taylor of London England, would willingly contribute with heart and gusto.

To all of you with the guts to admit your passion for carp fishing, hidden or exposed, I give my heart-felt thanks. For, without you, my book could not be published.

Dan D. Gapen Sr., publisher

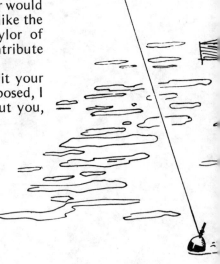

ISBN   0-932985-01-7

THE AUTHOR

Dan D. Gapen Sr., product of a wilderness heritage, might best be classed a caring naturalist, a man who intently cherishes the world of outdoors. He is a man on record, by quote, that fishing should remain a sport from which man must derive a zest for life and happiness within. And, that those who need to compete not dominate this sport in such a manner that the fun is gone.

Born April 9, 1934 on the shores of North America's giant Lake Superior, Dan D. Gapen Sr. is considered one of the nation's top anglers. To most, Gapen is considered the country's number one river fisherman.

Over the years Dan has fought desperately to save running water. Every facet of governmental bureaucracy has felt his sting. Gapen has been a staunch supporter of the National Wild and Scenic River system since its inception, a legislative bill he helped mold and instrument along waterways throughout the land. His favorite, the beloved upper Mississippi.

Within the covers of this revised edition of "Why Fish Carp?" Dan D. Gapen Sr. has passed along his knowledge, as well as others, on Carp fishing, its how-to's, where-to's and whys.

It is Dan's wish that once having read the pages of "Why Fish Carp?" you retain a few tips which will enhance your stringer weight next time out.

The Publisher

Additional "Why Fish Carp" may be obtained by writing:
Dan D. Gapen Sr.
1690 20th Avenue
Becker, Minnesota 55308
Ask for 'FREE' catalog booklet.

CONTENTS

...DEDICATION...
TO
David Conn
my dearest friend and fellow angler

cover fisherman Dave Conn
"for the love of a carp"

INTRODUCTION

"A booklet on carp Fishing?" You've got to be joking!"

These words of an ardent bass fisherman popped into mind as I stared at my freshly broken line. Minutes earlier my open-face reel had been screaming in protest to the frenzied rushes of a husky Mississippi River carp. It was like pitting Tiny Tim against Muhammed Ali. Though I played the burly fish slowly and meticulously, it snapped my ten-pound test line like wet spaghetti.

"If only my kibitzing friend had been here to see that," I thought. Moreover, if only it were possible for ALL of our nation's 40 million anglers to discover firsthand the brute strength of the carp. Unfortunately, too many fishermen continue to snub their noses at this outcast of the fish world.

Not so in other countries. In Asia the carp is King of Fishes. Emperors keep pet carp in jewelled tanks in some Asian countries while in Japan, carp is used as barter —— the larger the fish, the better its trade value. In Europe the lowly carp is highly esteemed by both commercial and sport fishermen while in England it ranks second only to trout as a game fish.

Years ago the father of American Angling, Izaak Walton, called the carp "Queen of Rivers." Apparently Sir Izaak recognized the

1

fighting qualities of the carp, something that continues to elude the modern-day fisherman.

The sole purpose of this booklet is to aquaint fishermen with carp and how to catch "ole buglemouth." It is not our goal to present the carp as something other than what it actually is.

Yes, the carp can destroy waterfowl habitat by uprooting aquatic vegetation. Yes, the carp muddies the water of lakes and streams. Yes the prolific carp can crowd out game fish. And yes, the bewhiskered carp is not the kind of fish you would have stuffed and hung on your office wall, even though a 22-pounder graces mine.

Angling today has evolved into a highly technical sport. Fishing has become too motorized, franchised and gadget laden. It has become too artificial, too competitive and even too expensive.

Whatever happened to the FUN in Fishing?

The carp, in a sense, can be your return ticket to fishing fun. Once you've hooked a carp, I guarantee you'll be hooked on carp fishing. With a powerful swipe of its broad tail, the bronze devil is off on a surging run that will test the finest tackle. Several determined runs and many minutes later, he *may* flop onto his side to be led to your boat. But watch out! The carp has a knack for rolling and flapping violently just as the net is swooping toward him. Many a fish has escaped at this moment to the dismay of the unknowing angler.

But the real popularity of the carp lies in its sheer abundance. Whether we like it or not, carp can be found nearly everywhere. So why not take advantage of that fact! If I were a city dweller and wanted to introduce my son or daughter to fishing, I would certainly make the carp our first adversary. The carp is easy to find and in many waters throughout America, still relatively easy to catch. Where normally an angler may find difficulty gaining access to a trout stream, landowners along carp-infested rivers or lakes will welcome you with open arms.

And let's not overlook the carp for its eating quality. I have dined on pan fried, baked, boiled, smoked, pickled and even french fried carp. In every instance the fish was delicious. Like that catchy advertising slogan goes — "try it, you'll like it!"

Likewise, I would urge you to devour the contents of this booklet. Just this once, shed the ugly stereotype you may have of the carp and heed the words of England's Fred Taylor (Chapters 4-8), considered by many as one of the world's top authorities on carp fishing and angling in general. Taylor has fished the world over including many of our states, but he still places the carp on a pedestal above all other fish.

"Why Fish Carp?" Fred Taylor has the answer. I challenge you to discover it. — **Dan Gapen, publisher.**

2

THE CARP . . .
A Biography of 'Ole Buglemouth'

The common carp (cyprinus carpio) which thrives in our lakes and streams is a giant member of the minnow family, the largest group of freshwater fishes both in terms of species and numbers.

There are three basic varieties of carp found throughout the world — — the fully-scaled Common Carp, the Mirror Carp and the Leather Carp.

Scales on the latter two varieties are irregular in shape and are completely different from the even scales of the common carp. Mirrors are sometimes fully-scaled but usually have patches or large, irregular scales on the lateral and dorsal region. Leathers may have from one to half-dozen scales dotted about the body. Some may be completely scaleless.

These different varieties undoubtedly spring from interbreeding with continental, quick-growing strains of carp that are reared selectively for food. Body shapes differ but fully-scaled Mirror Carp show no other biological difference from the Common or Scaled carp.

The Scaled Carp is predominant in America but Mirrors and other strangely-scaled carp have been caught in Arkansas and Oklahoma. These fish were probably fully-scaled Mirror Carp. Though few and far between, they lead one to believe that semi-scaled and virtually scaleless varieties will turn up in America sooner or later.

These unusual-looking carp may be the result of mutations. But more likely, they are the result of cross-breeding between goldfish and common carp. In big lake systems and reservoirs in southern states, goldfish are used as trot-line baits for catfish. No doubt

3

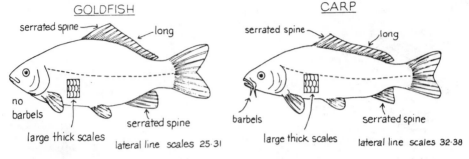

GOLDFISH — serrated spine — long — no barbels — large thick scales — serrated spine — lateral line scales 25-31

CARP — serrated spine — long — barbels — serrated spine — large thick scales — lateral line scales 32-38

many of these smaller cousins of the carp have escaped and increased in numbers over the years, leading to cross-breeding between the two species.

America's Scaled Carp is a robust fish, rather deep through the body and laterally compressed with large, thick scales. Its toothless mouth in sandwiched by a pair of barbels which the carp probably uses to sense food along the lake or river bottom.

The carp has a single dorsal fin. A strong, serrated spine is located at the front of both the dorsal and anal fins.

Carp vary in coloration. In cleaner waters they may appear almost silver but in most waters they are bronze or olive-green on the back, slightly lighter on the sides and white or yellowish on the belly. The lower lobe of the tail and anal fin are often tinged with red.

Average size of carp netted in seining operations is from one to three pounds but fish weighing from five to ten pounds are not uncommon.

A one-year-old carp may weigh one-half pound and measure just nine inches in length. Where food is abundant, a fish may weigh one pound the first year. Sexual maturity may be attained in two to three years. Carp are usually from 16-18 inches long by this time.

Carp can grow to a considerable size. A 90-pound fish was reportedly caught in Switzerland in 1902, though the authenticity of this report has been contested. Another fish weighing 86 pounds was supposedly caught in the Minnesota River near Shakopee, Minnesota, in 1906, but this report too has not been officially recognized.

The established world record carp by hook-and-line was caught by Frank J. Ledwein in Clearwater Lake near Annandale, Minnesota, in July, 1952. Ledwein was fishing for Northern Pike at the time. He had hooked a three-inch sucker minnow to his line which was resting on the lake bottom when the monster fish inhaled the sucker and steamed for the middle of the lake.

After a 15-minute battle ("it fought like a big snapping turtle") Ledwein was able to net the fish and lug it ashore. The fish measured 42 inches in length with a 31-inch girth.

Basic carp varieties include (clockwise from top right): Common Carp, Mirror Carp, Near-Leather (actually a Mirror Carp) and Leather Carp.

Carp move into shallow bays, stream tributaries or flooded plains and marshes to spawn in late Spring or early Summer. Once in these shallow areas, they go about their business of laying eggs with little concern for danger. Often their backs are exposed, providing an easy and inviting target for spearers and bow-and-arrow enthusiasts.

The prolific carp scatter their eggs at random over plant beds, debris and rubble. Eggs are usually deposited in groups of from 500 to 600 in an area roughly six feet in diameter. Large females may lay 500,000 to as many as 3,000,000 of the tiny, grayish-white eggs. The slightly adhesive eggs stick to debris, plants, or sink to the bottom.

Adult carp will do nothing to prevent predation of their eggs by other fish. Those eggs that survive hatch in from five to twelve days, depending on water temperature. Within four to five days the fish use up their tiny yolk sacs and at 18 days, the young carp may be nearly one-inch long. At this time they tend to migrate into deeper water.

Carp feed on nearly anything edible. Aquatic invertebrates however, make up a large part of their diet, including insect larvae, crustaceans and small mollusks. With their vacuum cleaner mouths, carp do much rooting along the bottom, often uprooting water plants in the process.

Feeding habits may vary with the size of the fish. In a study of lakes in southern Minnesota, stomachs of carp of all sizes contained 30 to 40 percent vegetable matter and 15 to 30 percent aquatic insects. Fish smaller than five inches had been feeding mainly on waterfleas and scuds. Fish between five and eleven inches seem to perfer aquatic insects. Carp have also been found to suck up the eggs and small fry of food and game fish.

Tests on blind carp revealed that liver extract, beef bouillon, other meat products, tobacco juice, immitation maple flavor, saliva and molasses are natural attractants.

The carp is a hardy, durable fish that can live in waters that will not sustain other fish species. Carp require little oxygen and can live comfortably in warm ponds and sluggish streams. In stagnant, polluted waters they suck in the oxygen-rich surface film which has been in direct contact with air.

Carp have a strong instinct for survival. They can survive out of water for long periods and withstand extreme changes in water temperature. Two biologists in New York State force-fed 1600 chemicals to carp under laboratory conditions. Amazingly, only 135 of the chemicals killed all carp tested.

And so, it looks as if America is stuck with this bewhiskered drifter, no matter how many fish traps are constructed, no matter how many lakes are treated with fish toxicants. And so, why not make the most of him.

2

CARP IN AMERICA . . .
From Hero to Villain

(Editor's Note: Much of this chapter has been taken from an article co-authored by Dr. John B. Moyle and Jerome H. Kuehn, both of the Minnesota Department of Natural Resources, printed in *Waterfowl Tomorrow*, U.S. Department of the Interior, publisher).

Early records tell us that Asiatic carp were first introduced in Europe as early as 1227. But nearly 650 years were to elapse before the carp found a home in America.

It is almost mind-bogling to think that America's tremendous carp population all began with just five carp, each near death after a long and arduous journey by steamer from Germany.

These survivors were among 83 shipped by J.A. Poppe of Sanoma, California, from Holstein, Germany in August, 1872. The five sickly fish were nursed back to robust health in private rearing ponds where they eventually spawned a new and highly successful business enterprise for Poppe.

By 1876, Poppe was peddling his precious fish to Game Departments throughout the country and including Central America and the Hawaiian Islands. In a letter taken from the files of the Minnesota Department of Natural Resources, Poppe wrote:

"I arrived here direct from Reinfeldt, Holstein, in August 1872 with five small carp six inches long. The fish were in a very precarious condition, one dying as I placed it in the water. In the following May the original carp had grown to sixteen inches in length, and the young fish amounted to over three thousand.

"Every fish that I can possible send to market here sells readily at one dollar per pound. Farmers who have natural facilities on their places for making ponds and who have access to canals or rivers communicating with large cities, can greatly increase their income with but small trouble and expense.

"There ought to be one person in every county who would raise choice carp as stock fish to sell to others to fatten for their own tables. It would be a cheap but sumptuous food and at the same time very convenient, as they are ready to be eaten at all times of the year."

Other piscatorial entrepreneurs pinned their financial futures on the German carp. Robert J. Pell of Pelham, New York in 1857 "had carp in great numbers" from stock he had obtained from a Captain Robinson of Newburgh, New York.

Wide distribution came in 1877, when the Bureau of Fisheries imported Scaled and Mirror carp. The reason, wrote Spencer F. Baird, then United States Commissioner of Fish and Fisheries, was: "Their instinct for domestication has already been established — and there is no reason why time should be lost with less proven species." So carp were brought here, propagated, distributed and planted with tender loving care.

The carp were obtained from Germany. Distribution to several states began in 1879; it ended in 1897. It was at a peak around 1883, when 260 thousand were distributed to 298 of the 301 Congressional Districts.

Thousands of requests for the fish came from enthusiastic sportsmen. Care was taken to obtain disease-free stock. They were amazingly healthy and prolific. One researcher reported 1.5 billion eggs on a 600-acre spawning area along the Illinois River in 1912.

But while the carp came as a hero, people soon began to regard the prolific fish as something of a villain. By the turn of the century, carp were thriving vigorously in lakes and rivers throughout the country — and they were causing damage.

As early as 1883, the increase in carp was accompanied by a great decrease in wild celery and wild rice in the shallower water of Lake Erie, which is warmer and shallower than the other Great Lakes and well-suited to carp. Milton Trautman in his Fishes of Ohio wrote that in 1899, two decades after carp were stocked in Lake Erie, 3.6 million pounds were taken by commercial fishermen.

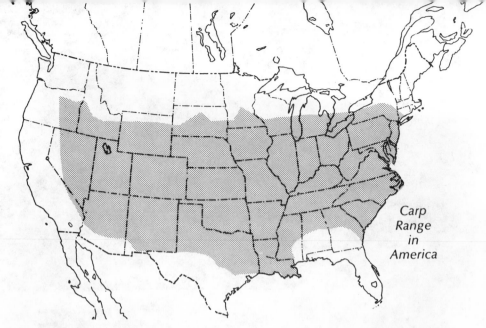

Carp
Range
in
America

A similar population explosion occured in the Illinois River where the commercial catch was one million pounds of buffalo-fish in 1880 but 22 million pounds of carp in 1896.

About 15 years after carp had been stocked in central Canada, Edward Prince, a Canadian warned: "German carp are nomadic in their habits and wander apparently aimlessly into all accessible waters, hence if introduced into any streams, will spread rapidly over the whole system . . . Like undesirable weeds, they have spread everywhere and it is practically impossible to limit their progress or to effect their extirpation."

Furthermore, American anglers showed no enthusiasm for carp.

Those who rate the canvasback as the king of waterfowl had a special reason to despise the carp because it ruined some of the finest "can" lakes in the country such as Lake Koshkonong on the Rock River in Wisconsin and Pomme de Terre in Minnesota. In these lakes the carp devestated wild celery beds and pondweeds which once attracted great flights of canvasback ducks.

The adverse reports prompted the U.S. Fish Commission to assign Leon J. Cole to investigate. He reported in 1905: "As to the relation of carp to aquatic vegetation, the evidence seems to be pretty strong that in general they are very destructive, and are probably, in large part at least, responsible for the great reduction of wild celery and wild rice that has been noted in many of our inland marshes in the last few years . . . It must be admitted that where there is a comparatively large number of carp in a pond the water is in almost constant state of roiliness . . . The only practical remedy is removal of the fish."

He was right. Carp rapidly became the dominant fish in many lakes and rivers. They did best in fertile, limy waters and warm, shallow nonstratified lakes, where they browse over the whole

9

Commercial netting of carp continues in about 40 states, though the fish is not of great commercial value. Total catch in the U.S. averages about $1.5 million annually.

bottom. Estimates of the standing crop of fish in such shallow, fertile lakes in the midwest often include 200 to 400 pounds of carp to the acre, plus about 100 pounds of game fish.

In an analysis of the problem in Wisconsin, it was found that the greatest production of carp, in terms of seining results, was from waters 10 to 20 feet deep and the lakes fertilized with domestic sewage had high yields of carp. In three such lakes, the average annual removal was 130.3 to 439 pounds an acre. Deep, cool lakes, however, often have small populations of large carp, which do little damage to aquatic vegetation except in shallow bays.

Lake Minnetonka in Minnesota, is a lake with many shallow bays. Its warm, fertile waters harbor good populations of game fish but the lake is well-suited for carp. It 1972, for example, Minnesota fisheries crews recorded an unprecedented seine haul in

10

which more than 225,000 pounds of carp were netted in a single operation!

Carp have been in the Midwest for 75 years, but they have yet to establish themselves to most waters of the northern coniferous zone —— roughly the northern half of Minnesota and Wisconsin. Part of the reason may be that barriers, such as high dams, may prevent migration.

A likelier reason may be that carp require a water temperature in spring of about 62 degrees to spawn successfully. The main northern limit of their range nearly coincides with the May isotherm of 55 degrees and the June isotherm of 65 degrees. The quality and basic fertility of the water may also be a factor, since the waters of the northern coniferous region are generally less fertile than those of the hardwood and prairie regions to the south and west. It was noted in 1959 that carp were still advancing at the rate of 20 to 40 miles a year in Manitoba, where the 60 degree July isotherm may be the northern range limit.

The greatest concentrations of carp now are in the Mississippi River drainage, where 16.8 million pounds of carp were taken and sold in 1969, and the eastern Great Lakes Region, where some six million pounds were caught. Carp are salable but are not of great commercial value. The total catch for the U.S. in 1969 sold for about $1 million, an average price of about 3.8 cents per pound. The commercial take in the United States has averaged about 28 million pounds a year since 1955.

Heavy concentrations of carp can cause serious damage to lakes not only by uprooting aquatic vegetation, but also by muddying the water itself. Large numbers of carp constantly roil the water and thus penetration of light is reduced and growth of submerged plants is retarded. Carp often are associated with heavy blooms of blue-green algae. The stirring of the bottom by carp and fishes of similar habits may keep nutrients in the lake bottom in circulation and may promote algae growths. The amount of roiling depends somewhat on the kind of bottom soil and is of least consequence where the soil is fibrous.

Changes in aquatic habitat come quickly as a carp population builds up. As the fish multiply, weed beds decline. Thick growths of pondweeds, water milfoil, coontail and other plants are replaced by bare mud. Water that was once clear becomes cloudy with silt. Fenced enclosures have been used to demonstrate the consequence of carp activity. The results are plain. Inside the fence, vegetation thrives; outside, the plants are consumed, rooted-up and destroyed as the carp burrow, root and churn. As long as they are present, water remains turbid, and recovery of vegetation is slow. Their removal often brings a spectacular clearing of the water and improvement for waterfowl.

Many instances of rapid return of vegetation, especially sago pondweed, have been noted in the Midwest after carp have been eliminated by toxicants or winterkill.

Control of carp has taxed the ingenuity and finances of conservation agencies for more than a half-century. Many States have engaged in seining and netting carp and trapping them during spawning runs.

The physical removal of carp from waters has been successful in reducing populations and benefiting the habitat and numbers of game fish in some places — usually in lakes that can be intensively and heavily seined over a period of years.

Many lakes, however, are difficult to sein and fewer carp may be removed than will grow up to fill the void in a year, so that little or no permanent effect on the carp population is achieved. In shallow, fertile lakes such potential growth of carp populations is high — often more than 100 pounds per acre a year.

In heavily seined lakes, there may be a change in the age and size of the carp population. In one instance, the composition of the catch following heavy seining changed from 13 percent to 93 percent juveniles. This is noteworthy for it is the younger fish that feed most heavily on aquatic invertebrates that are important in the diet of young ducks and game fish.

Screens and barriers to prevent carp from migrating upstream and infesting new waters or waters from which carp have been eliminated, have sometimes been effective. Floating screen barriers installed in conjunction with dams often are used. Carp lay eggs usually in the shallow waters of sloughs; exposing them to the air is an effective control if water levels can be lowered rapidly. This method has been used successfully on the Fort Randall Reservoir of the Missouri River in South Dakota.

Several kinds of toxicants have been used to eradicate carp. Toxaphene and rotenone have proved to be effective, but they are costly to apply and they kill fish of all kinds and many aquatic invertebrates. Toxaphene and similar compounds can also kill birds if used unwisely. And if just two carp — male and female — survive, it is too many.

Carp have caused many problems to be sure, but these fish have some redeeming qualities. Many shallow lakes would soon become chocked with aquatic vegetation were it not for their activities. In the South-Central states they provide anglers with considerable sport fishing. Commercial fisheries each year take carp valued at $1.5 million.

Carp have gained such a bad reputation that there is a tendency to make the carp a scapegoat for any and all damage to aquatic habitats. Other fish or even human activities may sometimes be to blame.

To corral a
carp . . .
A leap for free-
dom (above);
A carp's eye-
view of a trap
(left);
A typical
carp trap.

Furthermore, some kinds of fish that resemble carp may be blamed but are quite innocent. Feeding habits of different kinds of rough fish are quite different, as is their effect on the habitat. Buffalo-fish are large, native fish of the sucker family that superficially resemble carp, but they feed largely on flankton crustacea. Sheepshead, or freshwater drum, is a common rough fish of the Midwest that feeds on small fish and insect larvae.

The black bullhead, however, is a bottom feeder and may produce effects on the habitat — especially high turbidity — much like the effects caused by carp. The bullhead is often abundant in fertile, shallow lakes and can survive low levels of oxygen in water that kill all game fish, as well as carp, buffalo and sheepshead.

Indeed, the lowly carp has been a villain of sorts by destroying waterfowl habitat and food plants, muddying our waters and by crowding out some species of game fish. But like him or not, the carp is here to stay! So let us view the carp in a different light — as a resource to be enjoyed and harvested.

Mr. Carp is found throughout America in a variety of locations . . . rivers, lakes, backwaters, streams, bayous and wooded reservior bays. Water depths vary from a few inches to the deepest lake bottoms.

Carp anglers are seen to use cane poles, closed face reels, ultra light openface and even a casting rod and reel or two. Presentation grounds include river boats, weedy shoreline, rotten stumps and wading waters.

14

3

CARP BEHAVIOR

Carp are creatures of habit. They learn quickly, form a habit and provided nothing occurs to break it, will follow it for a long time.

They enjoy warm water, even though it may be too warm for them to feed. Carp have been caught in the winter in lakes fringed with ice. The first frosts usually mark the end of the carp season, however. In general, they cannot be expected to feed in water much below 50 degrees F.

The frequently-debated effect of weather on the fish is mainly, if not entirely, because of changes in temperature and in the oxygen content of the water.

Other things being equal, an increase in oxygen content seems to increase their appetite. The amount of dissolved oxygen is influenced by temperature, water depth and the degree of agitation, as for example, by wind or rain.

Other factors which affect the amount of oxygen in the water are weeds, which give off oxygen in the daytime and carbon dioxide after dark, and decaying matter which absorbs oxygen. There is less oxygen in very deep water then in shallow.

Let's follow the carp in a small, shallow lake during a typical 24-hour period in summer. Let's study the general pattern of their movements and see how different conditions modify that pattern.

At mid-afternoon, nearly all of the carp will be at or near the surface. Most will be in the shallows, for on this day there is very little wind, the sun is shining and the water temperature at the surface is well over 70 degrees. Many of the carp will be gliding slowly back and forth, some raising a glistening back or dorsal fin above the surface. Others will be almost motionless among the weeds. Few of the fish will show any sign of willingness to feed.

When evening arrives and the temperature begins to fall, the carp will show more activity. Some may begin to feed at the surface; others at the bottom. As temperature falls, there may be some leaping. A general movement toward the east side of the lake will begin, as this side gets the last of the sun.

If the sky is cloudless, the temperature may fall rapidly after sunset and the majority of the fish will make their way into deeper water. Some will remain near trees which prevent radiation losses, or a high bank which radiates heat stored during the day.

If the weather has been generally warm, and the lake contains a reserve of warm water in the deeps sufficient to maintain some areas at a temperature above 60 degrees F or therabouts, carp may feed there all night. Otherwise, they will cease feeding, but will spend the night in the warmest places they can find.

If, instead of a clear sky, a warm day is followed by a clouded sky, radiation losses are less severe, and the carp may remain in shallow water all night, usually feeding there.

Carp are likely to feed in shallows during the daytime if wind or rain keep the temperature on the shallows between 60 degrees F and 70 degrees F and by agitation, increase the oxygen-content of the water. If the temperature on the shallows is reduced below 60 degrees F or thereabouts, the carp will tend to move into deeper water which cools more slowly.

Most commonly, midnight finds most of the fish in relatively deeper water unless the night is exceptionally warm.

Just before dawn, the fish may begin to move to the edge of deep water nearest the west side of the lake, which first receives the morning sunshine. With first light a few will venture into shallower water on this side. This they often do from habit, even when the temperature fails to rise.

With rising temperature, activity among the fish increases and some leaping may again be seen. No one knows exactly why carp leap. It seems to accompany changes of temperature, and that the more rapidly such changes take place, the more fish are inclined to leap. Possibly, leaping may often be a preliminary to feeding.

A further increase in temperature attracts the fish towards shallower water, especially on the western side, until by midday they will again be nearly all on the shallows and if temperature has risen too high, no longer feeding.

Usually, rain or wind in the early morning will delay the emergence of fish from the deeps. If there is no rise in temperature, the fish will remain there. Whether they feed there will depend on the temperature. In a shallow lake, i.e., one which has no depths greater than six feet or so, feeding is unlikely. Deeper waters, however, may take longer to cool, especially after a spell of warm weather and since carp do tend to be creatures of habit, a trial at the western edge of the deep water may prove successful.

It will be seen, then, that weather affects the fish only because it affects the water; and that the direction of the wind, the state of the moon, the height of the sun or the type of cloud have no bearing on the matter except in that way. No particular wind-direction is in itself good or bad, and the lowering of temperature, whether by wind or rain, may start or stop the feeding of carp, depending on what the conditions were previously.

Similarly, the value of fishing at night is determined more by water conditions than by darkness. Carp fishing is often good at night in summer because the temperature may fall sufficiently to induce the fish to feed. This is especially true in small shallow lakes where such conditions may persist for long periods.

There are numerous occasions, however, when fishing at night is useless and daytime is much better. Other factors, such as the presence in the daytime of anglers or other people who scare the carp, all have their effect. If throughout the day, the carp are kept continuously alarmed, they may commence feeding only at night after the disturbances have ceased, though water conditions may be less favorable then.

Carp with full stomachs may often prove difficult or impossible to catch under apparently ideal conditions. Having eaten their fill, carp digest their meal, so that favorable conditions extending over a long period will result in fish feeding at intervals: the larger the fish, the more it will eat and the longer it will take to digest its meal. Therefore, the angler's best change is often at the beginning of favorable conditions.

There may be minor differences in temperature and the carp may react slightly differently from lake to lake or river to river in different regions of the U.S. But generally, this lore holds good. And it is a simple matter to look upon one corner or bay of a big body of water, and apply the lore accordingly.

In lakes with vast areas, a warm surface layer begins to form in spring and increases in temperature and depth throughout the summer. Carp aften feed in the surface layer and indeed on the surface itself, but those that have established themselves below that layer (primarily for reasons of food supply) experience little change in temperature for many months on end. This undoubtedly explains why anglers have caught Arkansas carp at zero air temperature in the morning and 70 degrees F in the afternoon — on the same day!

17

A FISHING CONTEST

A good start

Fun, but too small!

3rd Prize

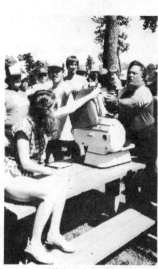

"Weigh-in"   *The "WINNER"*   *The day's catch goes home*

Dan Gapen hefts a 22-pounder caught on a brown Ugly-Bug.

4

HOW TO 'LURE' A CARP

The little brown Ugly-Bug tumbled through the morning air in a long, graceful arch toward shore. Its tiny white feelers, accented by the early glow, resembled the whirring wings of a dragonfly as it skitters over the water.

The cast was perfect —— scant inches from shore and a submerged log.

The soft "plip" of the lure striking water had barely reached our ears when a huge, scaley back suddenly protruded above the surface and hurtled toward the lure. The scene was vaguely reminiscent of the vengeful attack of the Nautilus which disembowled unsuspecting ships in Jules Vernes' classic novel.

Though on a much smaller scale, the on-rushing fish slammed into the Bug like a pro linebacker. Then, with a vicious thrust of its broad tail, veering away from shore and into the deep current.

"Big smallmouth!" came the cry from the other end of my John-Boat as Jerry McKinnis of ABC television's "Fishing Hole" scrambled for the landing net.

With McKinnis offering instructions and his cameraman Billy Murray busily exposing yards of film, my battle with the lunker fish became a back-straining tug of war. Minutes passed and still the belligerent smallmouth could not be seen in the swirling dark waters of the Mississippi River.

"It's got to be close to your Minnesota record for smallmouth," Jerry proclaimed. "I've never seen a fish smack a lure like that and fight so hard —— except maybe a bonefish or tarpon," he added as an afterthought.

The battle ensued for several more minutes before the fish began to tire. Slowly it gave ground until it was about two feet immediately below the boat. With a desperate lunge, Jerry plunged the landing net into the turbid water and scooped out the violently flapping fish.

"What the . . . It's a Carp!" Jerry exclaimed, his voice a blending of astonishment and laughter. "I had no idea they will strike lures!"

Prior to that balmy August afternoon on the Mississippi, I too, never dreamed carp would take artificials. But from that day on, lure fishing for carp has opened a new frontier in angling not only for myself, but many other Minnesota fishermen who float the Upper Mississippi.

The total amount of factual information regarding carp fishing with artificials could probably be written on the back of a playing card. Knowledge to date is based solely on the limited experiences of anglers like myself who have accidentally hooked carp on artificials.

There are several theories as to why a carp will take an artificial lure. In the summer of 1972, I guided Bill Scifres, Indianapolis Star outdoor sports editor and Indiana bait dealer Bill Hoffman on one of our "Old Man River Float Trips" on the Mississippi above Monticello, Minnesota.

Bill Hoffman toted along a batch of crawfish (crayfish) which he boasted would catch him twice as many smallmouth as other members of our party. He caught twice as many fish alright, but they were carp, not bass.

Throughout late July and August, the crawfish apparently becomes a staple in the diet of carp. The Ugly-Bug, of course, with its rubber legs and supple body, closely resembles the crawfish. And when it is jigged or twitched through the water, the Bug will dart forward, its legs whipping and kicking, amazingly similar to the movement of the crawfish. This mimicry is just too much for Mr. Carp and he takes the lure.

Of course, carp have been known to strike other artificials including daredevils, french spinners and bottom-running plugs. During the shad fly hatch, they will often rise to feed on dead flies and fly larvae on the surface.

How does one go about catching carp on artificials? Again, we must rely on limited past experience to find any answers.

This 9-pound carp inhaled an Ugly-Bug lure. Fighting time: One minute per pound.

On the Mississippi River, I have taken many carp where water spills over rocks at the head of large pools. Possibly the carp hunts these areas for crawfish. But I have also taken carp at the bottom and toward the tail end of these same pools. Smooth, fast–flowing slicks with the lure bounced slowly along the bottom will also produce fish.

While the Ugly-Bug and other artificials can entice carp to strike, the addition of live bait or some other tasty tidbit can greatly enhance fishing success. Lures tipped with a small section of nightcrawler, a worm or even pieces of corn are effective probably because they appeal to the carp's sense of smell.

Above all, spin-casting for carp necessitates a painstakingly slow retrieve because carp will invariably eyeball a lure before inhaling it. Allow the lure time to sink. It will fall somewhat faster than most natural carp foods but in the same filtering motion which often induces fish to strike.

This summer I hooked and landed a massive 21-pound carp (after a 26-minute battle) which gobbled up a brown Ugly-Bug on its way to the bottom. This instance and others have convinced me that not all carp are sluggish, bottom-hugging scavengers. They WILL rise to strike lures and they WILL attack a bait as savagely as most game fish.

Angling for carp with artificial lures can be both exciting and rewarding. Certainly, it is a new horizon worthy of exploration by the innovative angler. All sorts of new techniques, lures and equipment await to be discovered. It is a challenge that hopefully will not be ignored.

RIVER CARP BAIT

Black River Leech

Hellgrammites

A favorite . . . the Nightcrawler

Carolyn's doughballs

Colorful Jigs

5

HOW TO FISH DAM CARP

It was a typical hot, humid day in July when Dave and I turned our rig into the sloping, gravel driveway which led to Hub's Landing. Here we'd launch our 14 foot jonboat and motor the short distance up to Hastings Dam. Once there, it was our hope that white bass from the nearby river bottoms might be waiting.

Hub, a jolly, slightly balding marina owner, stood inspecting his broken down wood dock as we pulled up.

"Hi, guys! Dam water was high last week and just about took my dock out. Those guys from the Army corps of engineers can get screwed as far as I'm concerned," ranted our host.

Dave grinned and changed the subject by asking about whites.

"Lots of them up there last week in the high water. But, I don't know about now. Probably nothing there but carp today," Hub continued.

With the exchange of a few more pleasantries, the two of us paid our docking fee and shoved off. The sooner we arrived at damface, the better our chances at catching white bass.

As always, we headed for a known hot spot at the near end of the dam's lock gate system. Here, where water swirled around the cement wall's downstream end, many a stringer of whites had succumed.

23

Dave tied off on a pivot pin which protruded just above water-line on the open water wall. In a matter of minutes, both rods were seen to retrieve line and their attached 'Slip' lures. White bass love vibrating lead Slip lures, a manmade replica of their favorite bait-fish, the shad.

On cast three, Dave hit a small, pound sized white bass. My fourth cast produced a solid hit, a searing run, and then slack line. Upon retrieving the lure, it was noted that a large 'tarponlike' scale hung attached to the center treble. Inspection proved it to be a scale off a large carp.

"By gawd, Dan, I bet that one would have taken a while to land if you'd set the hook harder," Dave grinned an observing response.

"Yea, and I bet there are more of them below us," came my retort.

No sooner had the words passed my lips than Dave's rod jerked downward and line began to peel off. The fish ran downstream a hundred feet, then reversed himself and ran directly at the boat. Dave became hard pressed to control the situation.

"White bass, buddy?" I giggled.

"Hell, no . . . you know what it is! And he's big!" blurted Dave.

Yes, there was no question as to what Dave had hooked. Mister Carp now ran hard against the unknown adversary above. And there was no question he was having his way with my partner. Several minutes after a fourth and lasting downstream run was made, Dave's line slackened and suddenly went limp.

"Good . . . I didn't want to land that puckerfaced monster any-way," puffed my nearly exhausted partner.

"Sure thing, Dave . . . and I noticed you weren't enjoying your-self at all. That one will probably be the biggest thing you hook this summer, and it makes no sense at all to have boated him . . . right?"

It was true. As often is the case, large carp will give an angler a rough time when hooked and often out do any other fish in the water. It has been my opinion that pound for pound, the common carp will out fight any species which fights and swims beneath the surface. He may lack flair to explosively break surface water, but, stands second to none for brute power beneath water surface.

By analyzing our two pickups, Dave and I theorized the fish must be suspended at a water depth of 10-12 feet over a 28 foot deep bottom. Our 'Slip' lures (3/8 oz. size) would run at such a level under a normal retrieve. Thus, by lifting and lowering rod tips, an action was sent to our lures which would see them pene-trate up and down through the suspended fish. And, with the twin treble hooks mounted on a 'Slip', bottomside carp are easily snagged when lure retrieve is accomplished.

Each of us had a pair of fish on and off within the next few casts, but it wasn't until I heaved back heavily on my fifth 'fish-touch' that one of these unseen monsters was finally fought to a standstill and boated. On our hand scale he weighed in at 18 pounds, 11 ounces. A 'dam' decent fish on eight pound mono. The battle took nearly 25 minutes and left me completely limp of arm and bodily exhausted.

"Okay, so you landed one of those hogs. Now what?" chided my fishing partner.

"David, you've no respect for a fine fish. In Russia, I'd be a hero if I managed to catch a carp this big. And, in England there'd be a half page devoted to this massive brute in the Sunday London Globe," I bragged a response.

"Yeah . . . big deal. But, we aren't in England or Russia . . . thank God," came a gruff reply.

Mr. Carp can easily be enticed to a juicey nightcrawler during peak daylight hours.

There were a few more disparaging remarks about where my prize had been hooked, but soon David was into another fish, and he shut up.

Twenty minutes later, it was my turn. Even so, his carp weighed a mere 15 pounds, four ounces . . . not nearly an equal to my monster. And . . . his fish was hooked atop the back. Mine had been 'snagged' properly atop the right shoulder near its gill.

Dam carp fishing isn't a matter of just finding carp near the pools where they are seen to suck insect larva from the eddy's foam surface. Feeding carp, those working bottom structure, should be sought out in their normal feeding stations. Let's examine several by referring to the diagram in the chapter. Each station is marked via an alphabet letter.

At point A, a slow, backwater area near the wall side gate lock, carp hold just off the fast, white water flow of gate number one. They are seen to feed directly on bottom along the cement apron which extends down from dam face. Normal fishing techniques (described later in this book) will work . . . the best being a casting of dead bait up near dam face and a very slow retrieve toward one's self.

Due to corps of engineer regulations prohibiting boat traffic to close to dam face, this area often is deleted from an angler's reper- toire. If it isn't, boat positioning should be taken directly down- stream and in along the lock gate wall below the point marked A. Actually, the angler will be casting up along the lock wall face out near current break of gate one's current wash. Look for old

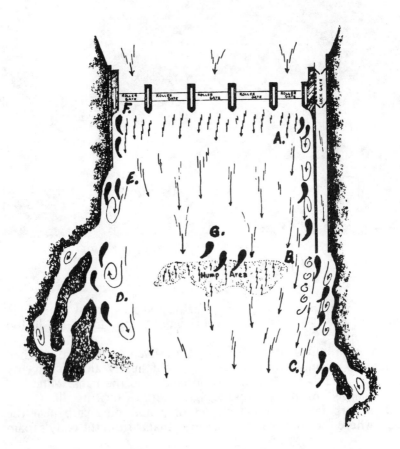

*Bait Walker Sinker -
a device which works
snagfree along dam
bottom structure.*

contruction eye bolts or tieoff rods, along the lock gate wall, to
tie your boat to. Regular anchoring can be most difficult at times
due to a smooth cement skirt bottom.

At the point marked B, two areas of heavy carp concentration
may be fished. The areas along lock gate wall just upstream from
B are the first. This station is one that sees a heavy movement of
carp going in and out, on and off dam face structure. They must
be fished directly on bottom in a 'still fish' technique. I find that
anchoring my boat above the suspected fish, casting my bait down
toward them, leaving it lie still on bottom, and waiting is by far
the most productive here. With fish coming and going constantly,
action can be fast. Use a rather heavy sinker rig such as a 2 ounce
Bait-Walker sinker to hold you in the heavy current which exists
here.

The second spot to be fished off point B is that area directly
at a point where lock gate wall ends. It is here, in a similar situation, that Dave and I caught our large carp at chapter's beginning.

This second spot may be fished directly on bottom where a
great deal of the fish hold or may be fished for migrating carp in
a similar manner used by David and I. It seems, due to man made
structure, I'm sure, that fish are seen to easily suspend at this
point. Possibly it is a gathering point for fish that then surge up
around lock wall and head for main dam face. I seldom have fished
such a spot and not found carp holding in large numbers 'off'
bottom.

That area downstream and along shoreline from point B may
consist of normal, earthy shoreline or can be rocky riprap. It
matters not! In some lock and dam areas this area is seen to be a
sandy beach with sharp, off shore drop in water depth. Such conditions exist along the Ohio River at a number of dams. Here, an

area of heavy carp concentration persists throughout the warm season. It is an area of multiple small eddies and back washes, easily identifiable by carp activity near shoreline.

However, as in evidence with salmon fishing, those fish seen to play at breaking water seldom bite. It is their cousins along the outer, deep side of these eddies that feed more readily and can be taken by fishermen. Such an area provides an excellent spot from which to pursue Mr. Carp from a shoreline position. Dead bait fishing with slip sinkers seems to be the key to catching fish here. A comfortable folding chair will also come in handy.

At point C, a smooth, rather fast, downstream—flowing water slick exists. Here, along gravel or stoney bottom, carp are seen to hold head into current, slowly working between bottom structures, feeding on critters such as hellgrammites and crawfish. Often fishermen are seen to hook these fish when jigging for walleye or smallmouth bass with light jigs tipped with natural bait.

There are two ways to fish point C structure. One is to anchor directly above it and still fish directly down upon it with long lines extending downstream from the boat. Another is to cast at an angle upstream and work your offering slowly . . . ever so slowly . . . down across the bottom structure below the smooth, fast slick water. Water depth at this point will vary but generally is found to be rather shallow . . . three to seven feet. There also may be a wing dam at this spot below many of our lock and dam systems. Such structure is fished exactly as described.

Point D is similar to C but with a couple of exceptions. Instead of having a heavy, fast slick wash over a gravel and rock bottom base as was the case at C, there exists at D a series of slow eddying pools. Here, along the hard bottom, carp are seen to feed regularly on both live and dead bait. Water depth, as in C, runs rather shallow . . . three to eight feet. Often schools at this point will exceed a hundred fish or more.

Unlike C, there often is a sure sign that carp exist at point D. They may be seen easing up along shoreline just ahead of the islands. In many cases, these shallow running fish are engrossed in the pursuit of rooting out crawfish for food. So engrossed do they become that they literally run themselves aground in hot pursuit.

Point D is often accompanied by a downstream wing dam . . . noted in the diagram. This, too, may be fished early morning with much success. Fishing technique in area D found to be most successful is a straight 'lay on the bottom' use of dead or live bait. In such an area I prefer to use live hellgrammites, artificial hellgrammite jigs tipped with crawler, or a small piece of potato and corn mixed.

Point E sees a similar type holding area to that area between B and C on the opposite shore. But, instead of a series of small eddies, this spot may have only a couple of strong reversing eddies

which hold carp. Once again this spot makes an excellent station to work Mr. Carp from the bank. Fish E in a similar manner to that described between B and C.

Point F is exactly like point A and should be fished and approached in a similar manner.

At point G there exists a downstream bottom wash hump, a by-product of almost every lock and dam system. It is a multi-species staging area but often produces some extremely large carp. This 'hump' rises to within a few feet of surface in many dam structures. It can last for 20 feet or as much as 200. Its size relates to current flow, dam depth, river's width and dam construction. No matter what its size, carp are seen to hold along the top side where bottom slants up toward structure's top. It is an excellent feed station for carp. In many cases, they use it just for this and once fed, retreat to a deeper holding area downstream.

The 'hump' structure at point G can be found 300 feet below a dam face or as much as 800 feet away. This, too, varies with the variables mentioned in the previous paragraph. It is best fished from an anchored point above fish shown in the diagram. Best baits seem to be crawlers, corn or hellgrammites, a variable which changes with the season.

Search for the hump area in any dam structure is best accomplished with some type of electronic flash unit which tells depth. However, it may also be found by observation. Wherever a hump occurs, water surface runs very slick above it and bursts into heavy ripples downstream from it.

Dave and I finished our day with too many fish on and off, sore arms and aching backs. And . . . no white bass! But, who wants to catch white bass when brutish monsters roam about?

Dam sites are a natural holding, feeding and staging area for schools of large carp.

The 'SLIP' lure.

6

CARP, KIDS, and LADIES

The question is so often asked of me . . . "Dan, how do I get my wife (or girl friend) to go fishing and enjoy it?"

It's an easy answer but one that when received, is not always accepted or agreed with.

The answer - "Take your wife out and let her catch all the small blue-gills you can manage to bait hook for. And, right when she's at the peak of excitement and when action is the fastest, insist you go home to mow the lawn, a chore she's been nagging you about for a couple of weeks. Right at this point, the key to making or breaking her future desire for fishing is created. You must go home, and you must mow the lawn!

Next, you postpone any future fishing outings with her for a couple of weeks, being that commitments have been made with the boys earlier that year. She'll understand immediately, especially after you promise to take her again next week. What was always a nagging confrontation in your lives now has become a complete understanding. You hadn't been boozing it up with the boys on all those trips before. You'd been too busy baiting hooks, landing bluegills, and trying to find one bigger than your buddies. Key to this thought is to make sure she doesn't catch a bluegill larger than a fifty cent piece her first time out.

Step two of fishing introduction to the wife is to now take her to an area where carp, any size carp, are easily seen and caught. Corn and worms will do nicely for bait. By using whole kernel corn right from her kitchen you now involve your lady friend more intimately in the process. All these years and only now does she discover that her kitchen has always been closely connected with fishing. Connected, that is, in more ways than those messes created when you decided to clean the catch and 'fry'em up' after a hard day in the field.

When selecting carp fishing equipment your wife will use, make sure you undergun her a bit. Six pound line, a too limber rod and reel with a slip clutch has always been known to jam up. Why? Simple . . . what you are doing is setting her up for the 'fish that got away' tale. It's always a good idea to select a fishing spot that has a certain amount of underwater debris that will enhance and insure the loss of her first really big fish . . . maybe her first three big 'uns.

Next, while allowing her to cry on your shoulder and tell her tale of woe, you might suggest she use your rod and reel for another try. Line test will be at 10 pounds at least, and rod strength of notable firmness . . . plus a reel with a silky smooth drag. Select an area, without mentioning same, void of underwater debris and instruct your protogee to place her offering.

With a couple carp landed, it is wise to think of something which must be done at home. Cut the outing short . . . always cut it short those first times out. Don't keep your wife out there too long so that her fishing experience might become boring. I'd suggest no more than two to four hours. And, always leave time in between before going again. Leave her to think about it a while. Let memories of the last outing mingle with the boring, every day house work chores. Take a trip or two with the boys in between your fishing outing with the wife. Soon she will be asking when she can go again. Instead of harping at you for leaving the yardwork chores undone, she will now be begging to go along.

Here are a few other tips which help. Always bait her hook until a time comes when she decides that she'd like to try. And . . . that time will come! If you don't make any fuss about having to bait her hook each time, she soon will become intrigued and want to. Liberation for women will have set in. After all . . . if men can do it, there's no reason she can't.

Never put the wife in a boat, especially your new bass boat, and head out across your favorite water bent on a hot bass hole some 20 miles via rough water. After a flashy burst of speed exerted by your prideful steed, the long rough ride will leave her bored, frightened, and sore. You only then have to cast 300 times to land a puny two pound largemouth bass to discourage her forever from the life of fishing. First time women anglers are not

THE BATTLE

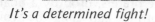

"Fish On!"

Finally . . . fish up!

It's a determined fight!

Up over the side fellow.

A prize carp and a proud lady.

*Who says that young ladys won't go
for ol' puckerpuss?*

impressed by your catching, then releasing, a pan sized bass. Especially after her arms throb with aches and pains from the number of casts she had to make at your insistance. The releasing part will most likely be the most unimpressing part of such a trek. "Why work so hard for a fish only to throw the undersized thing back?"

Never keep your wife or lady in a boat so long that she's forced to do a cross legged dance to keep Mother Nature at bay. Go to shore once in a while. Allow her to wander about in the woods. Nature will then find a way. If she prefers, drop by a boat dock where a ladies room is available. Both the above may be avoided if those first outings are short. I like to see the lady's first go at fishing confined to bluegills from shore and under two hours. From shore is particularly important when a child's first outing is being entertained.

All the above can be applied and related to when a child is taken fishing for the first time. Keep in mind that a child's attention span is short . . . much shorter than an adult's. First fishing outing for a five to six year old should entail no more than 30 minutes of actual fishing time.

All this may seem a waste of time to an avid angler, but it it's family fishing you're after, then such tactics as these discussed previously are necessary.

Carp become the first fish of any size that a beginning angler comes in contact with. And, for many, may be the hardest fighter any of these new fisherpersons come to battle for many a year. It's not too hard to catch a ten pound carp, but on the other hand it's very difficult to locate a ten pound walleye or bass. Even when the lunker walleye is taken, the carp will remain tops when fighting ability is considered. Thus it is that the fish of our first time

34

outings may last long in memory as the hardest fighter to prevail in our fishing world. Let this thought lead those of you who desire others to share your sport. When such is considered, there may well be a place in our fishing world for Mr. Carp. Beginning anglers, no matter what their age, remember those first moments and compare them constantly to any which come thereafter.

This chapter would not be complete without one other piece of advice to parents of those youngsters whose desire it is to fish. So often this author has seen a father or mother scoff at and distainfully disapprove of a catch of fish their child has dragged home. In most cases, it's our friend, the carp. What was caught in excitement, fought in determination, and displayed in pride is suddenly reduced to a scolding in displeasure.

Generally the child is told to get those horrid things out of the kitchen, to bury them in the garden, to take them back to rot along the filthy stream in which they were caught, or to hide them before some neighbor might see them. The child is ridiculed about not having any better sense about fishing and has his feat compared to that of some long forgotten fantasy of the father . . . a fantasy that over the years has seen immense amounts of weight increased on the stringer of bragging bass.

A pair come to boat.

What was once a feat of pride now becomes a thing of shame to the child. His desire to catch fish is lessened; his need to share such an outdoor experience with his parents decreases. What once may have been the makings of a father's fishing buddy now turns to other sports. Never again will fishing mean the same.

To place this last bit of advice in prospective, imagine the fight of a five pound carp to a 10 year old boy. Never before had he felt such power. Think about how that same child must feel when father takes him to the 'real' fishing world of bass and trout where he works for hours to catch one lousy 10 inch fish that couldn't fight its way out of a wet kleenex. And then the father has the audacity to proclaim this the real fishing world! Here's a boy who fought long and hard to produce three fish ten times larger than any of these 'real' species, and now his father is seen to brag in such a manner.

FISHING be damned. He'd rather take up swimming!

What better reward than a smile such as this?

OR THIS...

7

CARP AND CRAWFISH

It was a sultry, hot day in late July when the phone rang its rest-disturbing clattering clang. I'd been attempting a bit of rest on the front porch which overlooks Elk River bottoms in central Minnesota. There, a cool, moisture-laden breeze gently crept out across river bottom and helped alleviate the humid 95 degree temperatures of the day past.

"Yeah . . . it's hot, and you got me off my cool front porch seat. Whatever you're selling had better be good!" I arrogantly blurted into the phone mouthpiece.

"Yeah, yourself, Gapen. What I'm selling you'll buy for sure," came a cheery response at line's end.

It had been a long time since I'd talked to Bill Hoffman, a live bait dealer from Indianapolis, Indiana. Bill and I'd been fishin' buddies since day one. He loved to fish smallmouth bass.

"George and I want to come up and show you how to catch those record smallmouth bass you have in the upper Mississippi . . . how about it?" came the true reason for Bill's call.

Bill was always like that . . . going to show me how to get 'em on some new, squirmy earthworm about two feet long imported from South America, I'll bet.

"Sure thing, buddy . . . just like the last time, huh?" came my cheery reply.

The "last time" happened two years before when I was escorted down the Blue River in southern Indiana where we were going to catch huge smallies on secret 'jumping' earthworms Bill had acquired from a wierd worm raiser in Arkansas. Our biggest bass turned out to be not quite a pound, and it was caught on a jig and crawdad combo.

"Well, I tell you, fellows . . . it's hot and humid, and the fish are in tune with the weather. They're slow and unpredictable. But, it you want to and can be here in a couple days, you're on!" I replied.

"We're on the way, horse . . . and have we got a trick up our sleeve. Gapen, we'll blow you out of the boat saddle with this one. Get the boats ready. A coupla Hoosiers are going to show a Yankee a lesson," came a final note to our conversation.

Well, it wouldn't be the first time I'd been taught a lesson, but under the circumstances, I remained from Missouri . . . as the saying goes.

True to their word, my fishin' buddies arrived late the next day all primed and ready to go. When asked what new secret lie ahead, they just laughed and informed me I'd have to wait and see.

So it was that, on the last day of July, four of us began a three day float from St. Cloud to Elk River, Minnesota, a distance of some 40 miles by water. With the normal camping gear, fishing equipment and boat paraphernalia, there was loaded one special cooler that remained taped shut. At last . . . the secret key to catching huge smallie. When asked what lay beneath the cooler's

Carp for the bank fisherman can be a challenge.

cover, there came upon the faces of our two Indiana anglers a look of glee and selfishness. Dave and I would pay hell trying to get a look inside that box until the moment our guests deemed fit. Anyway, it would take a sharp knife and ten minutes of work to pry all the tape off so its lid might swing open. Maybe therein must lie the secrets of Pandora's Box or some fool thing like that.

Day one passed as I suspected it might. Dozens of small bass were caught and released . . . not one over a pound. A half dozen river sized walleye were taken at one 'upriff' run, making it possible to have fresh fish for supper. And, as on previous days, the temperature climbed high; the sun shone hot; and the humidity was nearly unbearable. The one thing this writer enjoyed were those few short moments when Dave and I were able to stray under the shade of an overhanging tree. Here, out of the sight of our over anxious partners, we were able to dunk a worm or two and come up with a bit of fast carp and sucker action. There also was that chance that a weary, old lunker smallmouth might seek the same comfort we did. Well . . . that's what we told ourselves.

Not until suppertime did Bill's magic box come into play. Both tents had been set, a cooking fire started and supper fish filleted when the two from Indiana began to unwrap yards of tape from the secret's boxtop. Whatever was in it certainly had to be valuable.

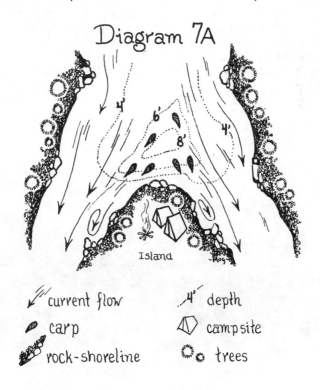

Diagram 7A

Island

↙ current flow   ↗ depth

🪱 carp   ◇ camp site

🪨 rock-shoreline   ❀ trees

Finally, after a bit more bullshit about how great 'whatever' was, the lid came open.

Ice! A whole layer of ice.

Below the ice lay several layers of newspapers . . . then a couple layers of brown paper . . . and a final layer of soft foamlike material. At last, the 'whatever' lay exposed to the human eye.

Crawfish! My gawd, they were nothing but crawfish!

"Bill, what the hell are you dragging brown crawfish all the way up here in such secrecy? We've tons of them for the catching here in the river," I stammered in disbelief.

"Nope, not these crawfish. They're special . . . really special. I raised them myself just to work the upper Mississippi. These are river softcraws shedded in my ovens at 71 degrees. They're all three and a half inches long and were impregnated with a special scent. These are super crawdads," came Bill's answer.

Hardly a word was said. Dave busied himself at the fire as fish fillets began to fry. I was at a loss for words. At this point in time it was best not to say anything. George giggled a secretive laugh and went about readying one of the special craws for rod and reel.

By now I'd noted the boxed crawfish had begun to move. Prior to this time I'd been under the assumption that they were dead. Bill explained.

"That's why we pack 'em this way in the cooler. There are three layers of craws. Each layer the same size from the same batch of young. Ice keeps them dormant. It's like hibernation in some ways. As long as the cooler lid is kept closed and taped, they will remain dormant a long time. We've kept them up to two weeks this way.

'float trip'

Crawfish (crawdads in Indiana) were the secret.

It was an excellent way to condition, keep and store crawdads. That was easily seen. Lowering the body temperature to near freezing caused the bottom crawlers to suspend growth and movement. There'd be no need for feeding them in that no internal functions were working. The idea was similar to that used when storing black leeches in iced water in your refrigerator. By adding just ice and dumping water, every three days or so, leeches can be kept throughout the summer months without loss.

"Well, you ready for your first lesson, big fellow?" yelled Bill as his newly hooked, special crawfish went hurdling through the air toward a deep current eddy edge.

"By the way, Bill, you might have a problem with those super special Indiana Imports. Up here, our carp feed on craws. They like 'em so well that they'll literally chase 'em up into the shallows and run them down," I commented as my friend, Dave, dropped a fresh hot walleye filet onto my plate.

George, now bound up in the same game plan, was next to wield his rigged crawfish toward the river's deeper water. Our two Indiana experts stood close together down from camp, their lines trailing off toward river's center. Finally, after a few anxious moments of wait, a pair of Y sticks were placed beneath the rods to hold them firm while their owners retreated, seeking supper.

George and Bill had just settled into consuming fresh walleye fillets when clickers on their reels began to hum. It wasn't an erratic clicking so familiar to those of us who live bait smallies or walleye. This sound was much more demanding, a steady, heavy clicking that wouldn't let up.

"I told you, Gapen. We both got one . . . big smallies I'll bet! Told you it would work," proclaimed a jubilant Bill Hoffman.

It took but ten seconds for the pair to retrieve their rods and brace themselves into a fighting stance. Dave and I stood atop the island's high point, eating fresh walleye and baked beans, awaiting outcome of the show below us.

Having set camp at the head of an island where the main river split around on either side may have been good to witness the setting of evening sun, but it did little to help our now floundering Indiana experts. Bill's fish had gone to the left while George's went right. Lines were crossed, then finally untangled in a fit of misguided action. Next both fish headed in close to shore and under whatever obstructions existed.

"My gawd, Gapen . . . aren't you two going to help. Bring a net or something," screamed Bill as he slipped and fell, righted himself and raced on.

"Dave . . . I'll bet money on the outcome. Two carp about five to eight pounds. That's what those two from Indiana call smallmouth bass where they come from . . . maybe," I giggled while finishing a walleye fillet and eyeing the one left on Bill's plate upon his departure.

"No bet, partner . . . those smallmouth bass run too close to shore and don't jump . . . a sure sign of a 'small mouth' alright but not the kind I'm after," Dave responded.

"Sorry, Bill . . . Dave says I should eat my fish filets, or he'll throw 'em out. You're on your own," I answered Bill's cry for help while snatching up the golden brown piece of walleye on his discarded plate.

A few minutes passed. There were a few words of discouragement to come drifting upriver from the direction in which our experts had departed. Finally Bill arrived, wet up to his you-know-what, mumbling about a big fish that got away. When Dave mentioned the fish-that-got-away might be a carp, he was rudely rebuked. That could not be so! It had to have been a big smallie. After all, it broke line off in an old tree stump, an ideal hiding spot for river bass. Maybe that was true in Indiana, but not so here on the upper Mississippi River.

Next to come was George. From the looks of things, his battle hadn't fared much better. Drooping chin and downcast eyes were the only answer we received to our inquiry. George would eat before telling his tale.

Not Bill! With the determination of an old veteran, moments after his arrival he was back at it, new crawfish and rig attached. This time he would await the monster. No Y stick was to be used.

Back at the fire George reluctantly told his story.

"You'll never believe it. You know . . . I fought that fish right up on shore before I discovered it was a carp. My gawd . . . I thought

I had the biggest smallie in the river. He must have weighed 10 pounds. Lord . . . Dan, I would have bet money on that fish being a bass. Bill is really going to be upset about his special crawfish. Do you know he's been raising that batch specially for this trip. He even put some kind of special scent in 'em. Good gawd, I don't believe . . . ." George's words trailed off and became indiscernible.

Neither Dave nor I had the heart to laugh. To alleviate the sadness of the moments, Dave began to cook more fish. I had managed to clean up both George's and Bill's during their absence.

Suddenly from below there came a voice, "Fish on! This time I'll land 'em and show you guys!"

Sure enough . . . Bill had once again set hook into what seemed to be a very large fish. And, once again there was a bit of battle directly upstream from our island camping spot only to see main encounter take place along the island's righthand side.

This time Bill held his own. A net was requested, and I obliged. Ten minutes after it began, with the netter up to his knees in water, a fish was netted.

You guessed it! Mr. Puckerpuss himself, a rather large fellow weighing around 12 pounds. Bill was shocked. I didn't have the nerve to say a thing. My old friend from Indiana might well have become an ex-friend from Indiana if I'd chosen this moment to expound my expertise on carp and crawfish.

Once the initial shock had passed, I managed to explain to Bill and George just why these upper Mississippi carp prefer to feed on crawfish.

Whenever a river system such as this one fails to provide a proper amount of aquatic vegetation, the carp species is forced to adapt to another food source. In the case of many river systems or lake waters, crawfish and hellgrammites are selected. Both are rather slow moving critters that work among the bottom structures where carp do a great deal of their food gathering. Thus, they become easy targets for these round-nosed, bottom rooting fish.

It was further explained that not all carp in our section of the country feed on crawfish. Wherever weeds abound, carp are seen to feed first on insects, then weeds and then any dead or decaying matter that might be available. They also relish food bits and pieces in the form of earthworms, slugs, small clams, and mullosks.

Camp that late July evening was set up in an area that may well have produced smallmouth bass. There was a dugout structure that is found above most river islands. Descending bottom waters are forced to split some distance above the island's uppermost point that in turn creates a churning action for any number of feet above the island's headwaters. (Look to Diagram 7A)

I had picked the camp spot for a couple of reasons. It had high land, and that upstream hole at island's head was an excellent spot to catch better than average smallmouth bass. Obviously, not tonight. But, the fact that carp had suddenly taken over a good bass hole isn't too unusual. It happens a lot in late summer when temperatures become unbearable. And . . . for the likes of me, I don't have a reason for such behavior. One day you're catching bass there; the next sees the entire structure covered with carp. It can last for a couple of days or a couple weeks. One thing for sure, it isn't a permanent happening.

To properly rig crawdads for carping, the angler hooks them through the underside of their tail in a similar fashion to that method used when challenging smallies (See Diagram 7B). They then are dropped some 18 inches behind a sinker, most prefer a snagfree rig like the Bait-Walker sinker on a trailing rig line.

Always remember to snap off the front claws as indicated in Diagram 7B prior to 'setting' your bait into position. Fishing procedure is simple. Cast the rig toward a likely looking spot, allow it to settle on bottom, crank up slack line and wait. You remove claws on the crawdad whenever you fish bottom with him while he's alive. Reasoning behind this is the prevention of his grabbing onto or clawing under some type of bottom structure. Few fish are able to root Mr. Crawdad out from under a small log or from behind a large stone. Once there, with his claws still intact, it may take an awful hard yank at rod tip to dislodge the ugly old devil . . . so hard that your hook can easily tear from his rather soft tail meat. Not only in carp fishing is this declawing necessary, but it is found to be an asset to the angler while pursuing other species of game fish.

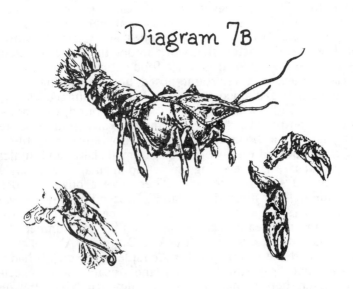

Diagram 7B

The crawfish Bill arrived with proved to be excellent carp catchers during the days that followed. Not one smallie succumbed to the charm of Bill's secret bait. That in itself was a bit amazing for crawdads are normally excellent smallmouth bait. Possibly the 'special secret' scent Bill had injected into his pampered critters was the culprit?

One last thing about craws . . . whenever possible, save the dead ones to fish carp with at a later date. A plastic bag and a slot along the frozen ice in your cooler will make it possible. By threading through the entire body via a long shanked hook, the angler is able to make decaying craws hold fast long enough for placement. There is hardly a bait better than a slightly decayed crawfish to entice carp with. In most lakes and rivers it is considered number one, especially on those tough-to-get lunkers.

If by chance the crawfish you use is of the hardshell variety, there is a procedure that should be followed. It's also a good idea to follow these same instructions if the crawfish is over 3½ inches in overall length. Snap off the tail portion of your crawfish. Once it's off, remove a small portion of the outer tail shell, leaving just enough to insert a hook into that will hold your offering firmly in place. See Diagram 7C. The outer shell is removed with good purpose. You must have smell to attract carp. As a matter of fact . . . to attract any game fish. By peeling off a portion of the outer tail shell, you are exposing raw meat which readily gives off scent. Hardshell crawdads have little scenting quality.

Diagram 7C

Snap off tail if body is over 3½ inches long. If light brown and orangish in color use tail with all its shell on.

Cut off portion of shell, as indicated, if hard of shell and blackish/brown in color.

Always hook crawdad via tail end (fan). Removal of shell allows scenting by hardshell crawdad.

After the initial shock of those first three carp, Bill and George were seen to try and try again. Each time a fish was struck, there were anxious moments of waiting while the first runs were viewed. Never once did the fish explode surface in the customary wild smallmouth bass action. Always the close-in shore run followed the first moments of flight. They took seven more in all prior to sunset.

Carp will be taken on those lures which best represent a craw-dad or smell like one. Such is the case of an Ugly Bug Jig in brown color when tipped with a worm (small piece of night-crawler).

The following two days saw Bill's secret bait tested several more times and always with the same results.

"Well, Gapen . . . what can I say?" Bill stammered as the jon-boats were pulled from water the last day.

"Not much now, old friend, but I'm sure by this time next year you two Hoosiers will have figured it out," I laughingly responded.

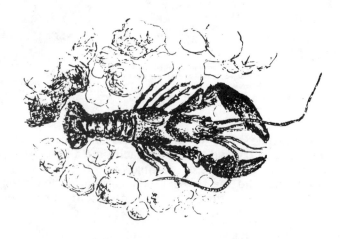

8

CORN AND CARP

I've been known to mention a truism about myself when questioned about those attractive fishing partners that often grace my boat. It answers something like this -

"I'd rather fish with an attractive lady than an ugly old man any day of the week!"

Yup, that's true and having done so over the years, there are a number of peculiarities about a lady and her fishing habits that should be mentioned when making note to Mister Carp.

For the most part, ladies really don't like to hold or handle the type of bait that might attract a carp or that other bottom fish called catfish. Sour worms, chicken liver and stinky dough balls don't do it for lady anglers. Well, at least not many women like to handle this type of bait.

However, the use of one of a lady's kitchen staples may be greeted with peals of laughter and much delight. Corn . . . canned corn . . . whole kernel corn . . . becomes a natural immediately when suggested. Most women make use of this vegetable every week and find its use in fishing rather fascinating. Hooking several pieces of fresh corn, plucked from a tin can, seems a natural act for a lady. There is no need to "hurt" a critter, attain smelly hands, or wash fresh blood from fingers. Corn is much cleaner and neater than other baits used on Ol' Puckerpuss.

Yup, I'd rather fish with a lady, and she'd probably rather fish with canned corn than wiggly worms.

Yes sir . . . and she caught it with corn . . . four pieces on a hook. How about that?   *"GOSH" . . . I did it, didn't I? How about that?"*

For those who've heard whole kernel canned corn does a number on carp, this information is correct. However, there are certain restrictions of how it might best be used to explain!

To properly approach carp with corn, bottom structure must carefully be selected. Open bottom consisting of gravel, sand and pebbles is best. Hard mud or shale ledges would be next with normal muddy bottom last. Never pick a bottom structure consisting of soft fluffy mud where moss style weeds are known to grow. Stay away from silt, no matter how deep it is. As with so many fish, carp prefer to root their food out or off a harder bottom area where it is easily selected or captured.

Fishing carp with corn can be done easily from a boat or shore. Often I prefer to be a bit lazy and work off a slowly sloping shoreline. If you fish with a lady, she may prefer such a setting also. Being able to get up and walk around can have its therapy on cramped muscles. Remember . . . this is a 'sit-and-wait' presentation.

When preparing to fish with fresh corn, there are several things which must be followed for best results.

First . . . always refrigerate your can of corn before leaving home. Carry it to the fishing hole in a container with your pop or spirits under ice. This precaution not only sees the kernels remain fresh but causes them to harden up a bit for better embedding on the hook. A can of corn left in the open, warm sunshine soon finds the kernels hard to retain on a hook. This warming will likewise see the corn's scenting strength dissipate.

Second . . . never place too many kernels on a hook. Use a 3X long shanked hook in sizes 8 to 4. Place no more than five kernels at a time on the hook's shank. If it's a number 8, an ideal number is three kernels. (See diagram 8A this chapter). When rigging corn kernels, implant the barb point through the hard, rounded kernel head.

Third . . . Some believe that the barb of a hook must be covered. In my case, I have found this isn't necessary. However, if the idea of a portion of your hook being exposed bothers you, why not cover it with an extra kernel. It certainly can't hurt.

Fourth . . . Like any other type of fishing with live bait, make sure your hooks are sharp. Single hooks left in tackel boxes often become rusty and dull from rubbing together. A few strokes with a wet stone will get rid of the dulling rust accumulation and assure you a firm hook-up. Carp are extremely sensitive and wary to the feel of fresh, sharp steel in their mouths, more so than most other species. Sharp hooks stand a better chance of staying in the mouth cavity by their very 'picky' nature. Often a hook-up is attained without knowing a carp has selected your offering.

Fifth . . . There have been times when freezing whole kernel corn prior to venturing into the field seems to add enticement. Freezing it and placing the kernels on your hook frozen seems to enhance the odor which is emitted. The softer and warmer the kernels become, the less attractive they become to Mr. Carp.

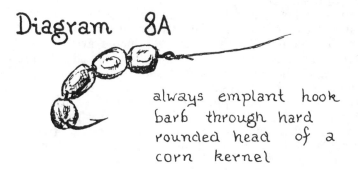

Diagram 8A

always emplant hook barb through hard rounded head of a corn kernel

Some will tell you to add a bit of marshmallow or one of the very small minature size white marshmallows between kernels. I've found this to help about 10% of the time. Mostly such an application is beneficial when lake or river bottom is soft. The marshmallow gives added lift to your bait, causing it to rise slightly off bottom (See diagram 8B). A second benefit would be the melting of the marshmallow gives a scent which seems to be attractive to carp. The one drawback with this is that an angler must continually add marshmallows as the previous one melts away.

Diagram 8B

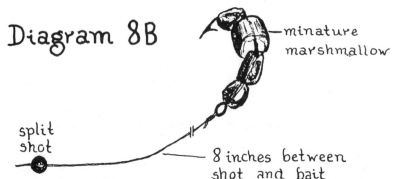

—minature marshmallow

split shot

8 inches between shot and bait

Use of canned corn requires the angler to maintain his patience. It's a sit and wait game. Once the sinker has been placed on the line, corn properly embedded on hook, and a likely looking spot casted to, Mr. Angler must wait out the arrival of the wary carp. To help speed up the entire process, an angler might consider pre-baiting. Doing this is simple. A day or two before fishing a likely looking spot, the angler opens a can of corn and scatters it along the bottom where he will fish. Two days and a couple cans of baiting corn will be all it takes to see carp begin to regularly use this area as a food stop. Bait corn can be scattered by hand from either shore or boat.

When rigging, use as light a sinker as possible. I prefer tiny shot or as small an egg sinker as is manufactured. For normal rigging, make sure your sinker is at least 15 inches away from the bait. There is one exception . . . if marshmallows are added to raise corn off bottom, shorten the distance between sinker and bait in half (five to eight inches). Though carp are known to take food 'up off' bottom, they are best approached as close to bottom as possible.

Ideal way to assure hook-up on the strike is to lower your rod tip as first signs of fish are noted, count one . . . two . . . three and set hook hard. First indications of fish at line's end come as a pair of 'tap taps'.

Some of the best equipment to work with corn comes in those long, wispy rods that reach lengths of seven to nine feet. Mount them with an open faced reel, and they're known to withstand tons of pressure. Selection of equipment can be accomplished best by choosing a live bait combo rod and reel.

To conclude this chapter, it should be mentioned that whole kernel canned corn can be used successfully everywhere in the North American continent where the carp species are found. It may not be as effective in certain areas as might be the 'hot' bait at a certain time. However, you can be assured it will catch you enough fish to make it worth your while trying.

Calm side channel river eddy provides an excellent structure in which to work carp and corn.

"Aint he cute?"

Even in Arizona, carp love corn.

A CARP FOR ALL PEOPLE

Young or old, male or female, carp are a fish for all people who thrill at the pull of a line and the bend in a rod.

9

MR. KING AND MR. CARP

It was the fall of 1984 when I lay to rest an old hunting buddy. And, while memories are very fresh and the heartache the toughest, I thought it appropriate to place in print a short dedication.

Timing was likewise relevant, seeing our waterfowl season was about to open. My friend lived to hunt waterfowl. Ten and one half months out of the year were waited out in anticipation of that six weeks in which retrieving of the wily waterfowl became his joy.

Yes, KING, my old black lab passed on late one frosty September morning. He did so in a manner that was customary to his theme in life. Watching while I loaded my car for a trip to Churchhill, Manitoba where photos of white bears and a goose hunt waited, the ancient dog dragged himself to his feet as my cased shotgun came into view. Upon reaching an erect position, he attempted to move toward me. Dying legs refused to respond. His cataract ridden eyes glazed over at the very moment my hand touched his muzzle. King died on his feet in a last attempt to respond to that inner instinct bigger than even he. Shotguns, cold water, and retrieving of waterfowl had been his way of life. True to his breed, King remained faithful to the end.

Perhaps there were clues to his impending death. He was digging holes in the yard . . . deep, deep holes . . . as if he knew and was compelled to dig no matter how hard it was on his old, arthritic body. Maybe he knew something I didn't for the holes became deeper day by day no matter how intense the punishment for digging . . . no matter how much I tried to stop him.

Those of you who have owned a dog and have lost him will understand why this chapter must be written. It is very hard to write. The paper blurs; the mind wanders; the emotions swell; and future hunts dim.

King was with me just over 14 years. I received him from a friend when he was eight months old. Nearly 15 years is a rather good lifespan for a black labrador who never spent a day of his life indoors and recovered from a very bad bout with heart worm some six years ago. In human measurement of time, that's about 100 years old.

This angler had better move that fish in within range of Mr. King or suffer the possible dousing of water which will surely follow.
Up and over . . . that's better!

As many times as the ol' dog plunged his mouth over a surfacing fish, never once did he appear to have been stabed by dorsel fin spines.

There are other things you might like to know about this old hunting buddy of mine. Until a week before his death, that old coot was chasing Wapsi, my six year old female lab, in an attempt to leave his mark on dog immortality via a son. If I ever had any doubts about such things . . . as they relate to age . . . King certainly gave this writer hope!

That old man had some other characteristics which, now that I think about it, weren't so great. He was damn stubborn at times. It was never his great desire to hold a dead duck in his mouth for long. You'd better be there when he hit shore or be willing to mark the spot where he did his first shake. That's where the duck would lie. And there was that matter about too many cold water retrieves. Unlike his wife, Wapsi, that old man would break ice and make about seven or eight icy water retrieves at which point he'd refuse to go again until he'd had a chance to warm up. Wapsi, on the other hand, would hit the cold water until she dropped.

I never broke King of running rabbits. In later years he got craftier at it and would only begin a race when out of my visual and hearing distance. There was something about a bunny he just couldn't resist.

On the other hand, I remember other times and places when my old friend and I shared skies full of waterfowl and days fresh with nothern winds when bluebills broke across a Manitoba pass at 100 miles an hour. I think of those numerous times I missed my shot when the old dog never said a word . . . I think of a day, years ago, when he did break ice 27 times to retrieve huge, nothern mallards for our entire party . . . I think of nearly mile long water retrieves when a wounded mallard all but got away . . . and I think of those times when his reserved need for attention caused his muzzle to wander between my hand and my wader leg.

Yes, King may have been a bit stubborn, but he was a gentleman and a rather classy individual.

In the end, those last three months, my friend suffered immensely from arthritis and generally failing health. Another winter he would not have made. But, it had been Wapsi's hope and mine that he might have stayed long enough for one more opening. Though he'd not have been able to retrieve again, just being there might have been enjoyed. Even old men can dream and remember days gone by, can't they?

I opened at the Ol' Forty hunting acreage that year of '84 . . . Wapsi and I. King was there with us. You see, he rests upon an island where a pair of nesting honkers make their residence. That seems appropriate. The stubborn old man can worry the devil out of their offspring for many years to come.

I'll miss you, King!

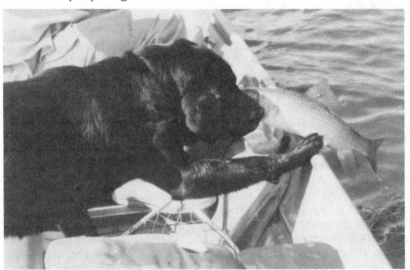

There were those times when certain species came hard.

Yes, King is gone, but never gone are those memories of his antics . . . antics that involved that old man in many a fishing excursion with his master.

King was always hot to chase carp when they were seen to travel the shallow backwater areas along the Elk River along those bank we lived. There was something about these ugly, yellowish-orange, puckerpuss mouths that King just couldn't resist chasing when they rippled surface. He never caught one, but never refused this challenge either. I've seen King spend an entire afternoon racing back and forth through the water in pursuit of just one solid bite.

This need to chase carp may have been enhanced by numerous carp fishing expeditions when King accompanied me. From a key position atop the flat front deck of my Alumacraft jonboat, King was able to do more than chase his round-eyed foe. King actually was able to reach down and 'get-a-hold' of Ol' Puckerpuss and lift him in. The first time it happened I nearly fainted. That first carp weighed a mere seven or eight pounds, had fought a stubborn battle and was lying exhausted on surface, awaiting disengagement when Ol' Kinger gathered enough courage to attempt a retrieve. King had followed the battle from beginning to end, just as always was the case, jumping about our boat's front end in an attempt to maneuver into a better viewing position. This time, instead of smelling his quarry, King gently lowered mouth down over my fish and lifted. Much to his delight and with eyes lit up, King lifted the carp aboard. There was the normal amount of fish tail thrashing which he took in stride by standing astraddle of the "fetched" prize. Once all became quiet, King turned and grinned. He was three years old.

Its time for one more . . . "I'm ready, get em up guy."

Jim Whitney, of St. Louis Missouri, eagerly awaits a turn to observe the smallmouth bass King has retrieved and will drop if only someone will open the livewell lid.

From that day until his death the old boy loved nothing better than to take his rightful place in my fishing boat and perform duty as a landing net. There have been many times when carp in excess of 15 pounds came popping to surface that saw my old dog struggle with all his might to see them aboard. Never did he fail me. Somehow he always managed to drag, jerk, pull or horse the giant puckerpusses in. Once aboard, there always came that wondering look back at his master, seeking approval. And, each time I acknowledged "good boy!", he'd grin.

King's fame as a fish retriever became better known one week-end in 1980 when an old friend, Jim Whitney of Peabody Coal Company, came to fish the upper Mississippi River with me.

"Dan, I've two black labs at home who love to lie around in the sun while I fish. Does King enjoy fishing? If so, let's take him along," my friend quiried after being introduced to my friendly labrador.

I giggled and agreed. Jim was about to get the shock of his life. As luck would have it, Jim's first fish was a 12 pound carp that put up a devil of a battle on light open face spinning outfit. As the fish struggled nearer the boat, King became more aggressive in an attempt to position himself for the eventual retrieve. Jim, of course, was completely unaware of why this labrador might act so strangely.

"Dan, King acts like he wants to retrieve my fish. Is he always this way?" questioned my companion in a puzzled response to the dog's actions.

"Just watch . . . that old dog will show you a trick or two," I giggled.

Jim's eyes darted back and forth between fish and dog. His actions denoted a bit of uneasiness.

It was when Jim's 12 pounder first broke surface that Kinger struck. Jim was in no way prepared for it. He nearly lost his rod as King's head struck the big carp directly behind the gills. With one fluid motion, fish, water and King's outstretched head came back across boat gunnel.

"My Gawd . . . that's the wierdest thing I've ever seen . . . a fish retrieving labrador! Gapen . . . you're something!" came the startled response.

"Not me, Jim . . . King!"

As with all before . . . and after . . . Jim Whitney could hardly believe his eyes. There really was such a thing as a fish retrieving dog. Later that day Jim was to become even more startled when King leaped a mere ten feet through the air only to land on a 4½ pound smallmouth bass at line's end. That incident saw the line break, but the fish was saved as Kinger proudly returned to boat with prize in mouth. Yes, the old dog often would become impatient while the angler fought a fish near boat's end and being able to stand it no longer, dive gracefully through the air to land on and retrieve the hooked fish.

In the case of Jim's largest-ever smallmouth bass, Jim had insisted that King do the honors. King probably just misunderstood when Jim had wanted it done . . . thus the premature leaping dive to capture the fish.

It was on that day that King earned a nickname that has lasted in my fishing circles till this day. Whitney decided to call my faithful, old fishin' retriever "The Black Landing Net".

IT TAKES ALL KINDS TO CATCH
"CARP"

*In this and succeeding chapters, English author-conserva-
tionist Fred Taylor shares with us his country's love affair
with the carp. Taylor, who has caught fresh and saltwater
game fish the world over, — including the United States —
presents the carp as it really is: a muscular, tackle-busting
fish that when properly prepared, can charm the taste buds
of the most discriminating Epicurean.*

*He also provides a wealth of information on carp fishing
techniques and helpful hints to lend even more success and
excitement to our pursuit of the wily carp.*

*Taylor, in turn, attibutes much of his information to
Richard Walker of Great Britain, holder of the British carp
record. His text contains extracts from Walker's book "Still
Water Angling" which are included with Mr. Walker's per-
mission.*

10

THOUGHTS ON CARP FISHING

I have travelled through and around some
26 of the United States during the past ten
years and I've fished for carp in most of them.
I've been called a crazy Limey and worse,
but I've made alot of friends, had alot of
fun *and* caught a lot of carp because I
wanted to.

The more I think about it the more I'm
convinced that the average American angler
doesn't realize how lucky he is!

Now, don't get me wrong. I've fished for
bass and crappie, walleye and coho, northerns
and lake trout, rainbows and brownies, and
I've caught them all.

I *know* what effect a great influx of carp
can have on waters holding these fish and how
game fishing can suffer because of it. Never-
theless, many waters in the U.S.A. already
have big carp populations and nothing is going
to change that. You've got the carp and you're
stuck with him. So why not make the best of
him?

England's Fred Taylor and his beloved carp . . .

Like I say, you don't know how lucky you are. Would you believe that in England, carp are rated very highly as sport fish?

We actually carry out big restocking programs in order to maintain stocks in our sport fisheries.

We go to great lengths and spend countless hours fishing for them by day and night.

We are happy to get *one* big carp during a weekend's fishing. And would you believe that we put many of them back to grow bigger and fight another day? And why not? Old buglemouth is one heck of a fighter!

It is the carp's fighting ability that we in England find so exciting and why I have been bringing over parties of English anglers to fish for American carp.

I know that, generally speaking, the methods used to catch carp are very much sit-down-and-wait-for-a-hit affairs, but I sometimes wonder if that's a bad thing after all. In this busy old world with its noise, speed and anxiety, what is wrong with "sitting a spell" on a quiet undisturbed bank to fish for carp?

They're exciting and relatively easy to catch, plentiful and good to eat. Fishing for them can be suspenseful, thrilling and relaxing at one and the same time; so what more could you ask?

I have a simple philosophy. I don't care what is on the other end of my line as long as it's pulling its weight and trying to get off! And I've always lived up to my promise that whatever fish decides to hang on at his end, I'm never going to let go of mine! The closest I've come to it has been while carp fishing.

Carp in the U.S.A. are not much different from the carp in England except there are more of them. This means the American angler can expect a lot more action. And that can't be bad.

There are many situations in the U.S.A. where carp are almost too easy to catch, but there are others where a lesson or two have been learned. Then a little guile and cunning become necessary to deal with slightly more sophisticated fish.

I doubt if American carp will ever learn as many lessons as the English carp already have (we've been catching 'em and putting 'em back for years)*. So, it's safe to say that methods designed to deal with English carp will certainly work in America. My experiences bear this out at any rate.

The British record carp weighed 44 pounds. It was caught by design and not by accident by a dedicated and brilliant carp fisherman who designed rods, tackles and methods to deal with what was then regarded as an almost impossible fish to catch. The fish was kept alive in the London Zoo Aquarium from 1952 until 1972 when it died at the age of 35 years.

Richard Walker, the captor and my very close friend, taught us all to appreciate the great skills of carp fishing, to convince ourselves that carp *were* worth fishing for, and that life was indeed *not* too short to spend some of it in their pursuit.

---

*In the U.S.A., some states have regulations against returning carp or other rough fish to water after they are caught. Be sure to check with state and local laws.

11

BASIC TACKLE

Basic tackle for carp varies little from the basic equipment used for other fish. Certain refinements and slight differences are worth considering, however.

You *can* catch carp with a five-foot, solid spin-casting rod and a cheap reel. But when the chips are really down and there's a big carp on the business end, these outfits are liable to fold up. They may not break but the rod buckles under the strain, takes on a U-shape and control over the fish escapes.

Good fish are lost and left trailing yards of monofilament because cheap, closed-face reels have ground to a halt under pressure. Ultra-light fanciers meanwhile, lose fish after fish by trying to beat them out of a snaggy water on two-pound test line. This, to my way of thinking, is sportsmanship at its worst!

"Give the fish a chance," they say. A chance to do what? To escape and spend days

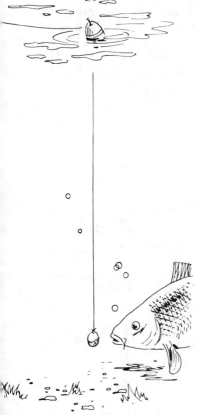

trailing 50 yards of nylon around the lake, a danger to bird life and a source of annoyance to other fish? A chance to make other carp spooky and ruin the sport for other anglers?

I do not want to "horse" fish out of the water. I want to hook them on tackle that gives me a good chance of landing them. That is why I use the best possible equipment and tackle I can afford and give a lot of thought to each particular situation.

Carp will test tackle to the utmost and it is essential to have the right tools for the job in hand.

The rod may have to be a compromise because of the different tasks it has to perform. It has to be able to cast a very light bait, often a very soft bait, a long distance. At the same time, it must have enough backbone to deal with a 20-pound fish going like a bat out of hell for the tree stump.

Special cane rods were developed in England for this purpose. Rods that would cast a one-ounce weight 100 yards and handle fish up to 40 pounds. Later, glass versions of these ten-footers were produced for the same task.

There are many suitable rods. The best are those with a soft and progressive action which cast well and pile on the pressure when necessary.

The choice of reel depends upon the individual. It should have the following features:

It must be capable of holding 100 to 150 yards of 12-pound test line.

It must be capable of recovering line quickly when a fish races towards the angler. It must have easy and comfortable means of applying drag, preferably by finger pressure, to a running fish.

American bait casters have these qualities but it is sometimes difficult to let a biting fish take line without resistance or over runs. Most have good line capacity and are completely reliable, but are not the best for casting light baits. For these reasons I prefer to use a medium-sized, open-face spinning reel.

Line strength of course, depends upon water conditions and size of the fish. I have never

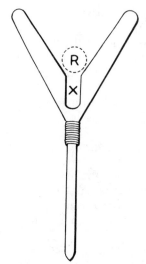

Rod lies on (R)
Line passes through X

had to go higher than 12-pound test and I will not risk anything less than 6 pounds for reasons already stated.

Hook size should naturally match the line strength being used. Wire thickness should also be considered. You cannot, for instance, drive home a size 2/o hook with a 6-pound test line. At least you would be lucky to do so in a carp's leathery lips.

The hook should be thin wired (but not those soft wire crappie hooks which are designed especially to straighten and pull free of underwater stumps. To use such a hook would be courting disaster!) It should be sharp, slightly offset and if possible, straight-eyed. It should be big enough to accommodate the bait and it should be tied directly to the reel line with a half-blood or clinch knot.

Rod rests can be made from branches, but if possible, carry permanent rests which allow for free passage of line.

A landing net is essential. It doesn't matter what brand or material as long as it is big and deep in the mesh.

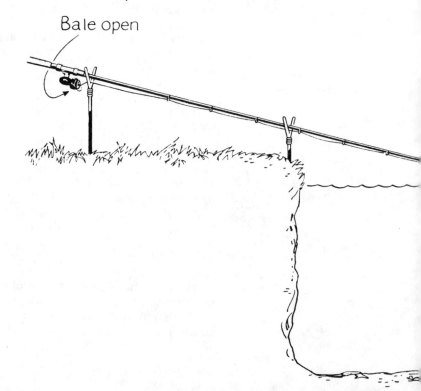

Bale open

12

FISHING TECHNIQUES

Carp normally do not school like crappies or bluegills but there are occasions when they gather to exploit a certain food supply.

Where fish are cleaned daily and the guts, eggs and livers are washed into the lake below the cleaning area, there are bound to be large numbers of carp and catfish. Why these areas are not fished during the heat of the day when the bass are strictly "off", I shall never understand! Isn't it much better to catch carp than *not* to catch bass?

There are plenty of carp for the taking but they are *accumulations* rather than natural schools. In fact, it is not uncommon to observe carp feeding in different ways in different parts of the lake at the same time of day.

It is a simple matter to bait with a piece of fish roe in an area regularly "chummed" with fish guts and wait for a carp (or catfish) to take hold. However, it is not as easy when the natural food supply comprises small worms or larvae which the carp dig out of soft mud. It is often difficult to convince carp that anything larger is worth eating. In recent years a few dedicated American fly fishermen have learned to catch carp on carefully presented nymphy. This is clever fishing and worthy of more thought and exploitation by others.

Generally, the only way to catch these furiously-digging and completely pre-occupied carp is to try and wean them over to something else. The American idea (completely unheard of until recently in England) of using soaked corn is one of the best.

The individual grains are small and have a smell about them which even if they don't attract carp, can hardly be overlooked! It is possible, by introducing enough kernels over a long period, to persuade the carp that corn is as good to eat as larvae or other small underwater creatures.

*Chumming or groundbaiting attracts carp and also introduces them to the bait you propose to use. Where it can be carried out for a period of several days, fishing over a baited area is likely to prove more profitable than trying to locate the fish. Let the mountain come to Mohammed, so to speak.

So, all that is needed is a lake bottom contour which, allied to observations of the lake and prevailing weather conditions, ought to be where carp can reasonably be expected. Failing any obvious indications, an area should have shallows which drop off *gradually* into deeper water.

If possible, locate a mark on the opposite bank (tree, building, etc.) and aim at that mark each time the "chum" in introduced. Handfuls of corn, bread, meal, fish offal or whatever substance if being used, may not all go the same distance. But they should go in the same *direction*. And the hookbait, when it is presented, should follow the same line.

These are basic carp fishing tactics. It doesn't matter too much what you use to

*Some states have strict regulations against depositing any "garbage, rubbish or offal" in public waters. Such laws may prohibit the angler from chumming with corn, potatoes or chopped fish. Check with your state or local laws.

bait up an area. I have had success with stale bread, chopped fish, corn and meal mixtures.

Hookbaits are most common and there is no real need to mix up scented or sweetened concoctions to interest carp. I *have* caught them on mixtures of wheat flakes and strawberry jam in America and I *have* caught them on honey flavored paste in England. But usually, a loaf of bread is more than adequate.

Where small fish are a problem, and where the bottom is of soft weed or mud, it may be necessary to present another bait in a different way. We will look at these situations later.

Meanwhile, for the purpose of getting started at this fascinating game, it is only necessary to take a piece of *new* white bread from the middle of a slice. Pinch the tidbit onto the hook so that the edges remain fluffy and cast it along the line to settle among the already-introduced mashed bread "chum". The hookbait becomes the "plum" piece, of course.

White and attractive, the morsel is unlikely to be overlooked by a foraging carp. Naturally, if the "chum" comprises corn, fish, offal, etc., the hookbait should be a choice portion of the same foodstuff.

The hook, which may range in size from No. 6 to No. 2 (there's seldom need for anything larger), is tied directly to the reel line. There are no lead or bobber attachments for this basic style of fishing.

Bites *can* be registered on the rod tip if desired, but rods *can* also be pulled in and disappear completely. It is advisable to allow for free passage of line by opening the bale (in the case of a spinning reel), or putting the free spool mechanism into play (in the case of a bait-casting reel).

Free passage of line also helps on those rare occasions when carp behave in a somewhat finicky fashion and refuse to hit hard. (I'm referring to U.S. carp now, of course. English carp *never* hit hard.) Somehow the lack of resistance encourages them to swim off confidently with the bait. When the line is seen to strip off the spool, it may be assumed with a degree of confidence that the bait is at least in the fish's mouth!

The "BATTLE"

Often it will take a pair of hearty anglers to land a hefty carp

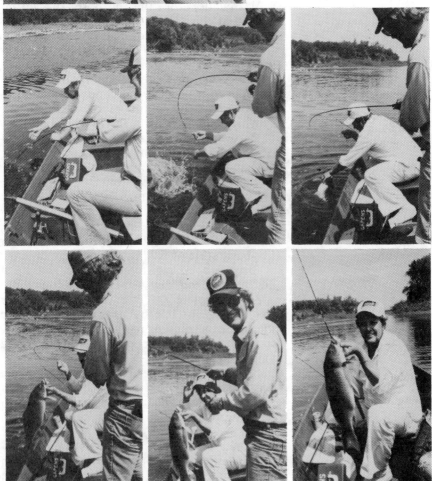

Ol' Puckerpuss . . . the Prize!

14

BAITS AND HOW TO USE THEM

If carp are known to inhabit a certain spot, *if* the bottom is relatively clear and weed free, *if* there is no layer of soft mud and *if* there is no likelihood of small fish being troublesome, the simple procedure of baiting and fishing described in the previous chapter will stand more than a fair chance of succeeding.

I prefer to fish with simple bread baits because I have seldom found it necessary to use anything more exotic. Fish have local preferences, however. I am familiar with a certain stretch of the St. Joe River in Michigan where I have been unable to catch carp on anything other than night crawlers.

In Illinois, there is a lake where the local preference is for a paste containing alfalfa and burbon (what a waste of good whiskey!), and in certain parts of Oklahoma, the carp's cuisine is soaked sweet corn (probably because they have been educated to it).

There are many situations where it is essential to educate the carp into accepting certain baits in order to overcome special problems.

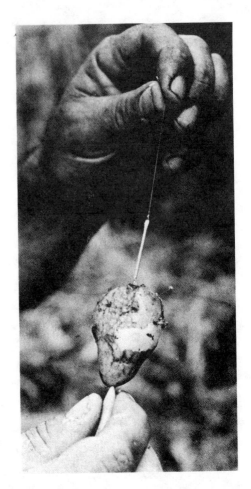

Baiting with a boiled potato.

Where carp are used to bread and baits derived from bread, there often arises the problem of small, unwanted fish. These can prove such a nuisance that it is sometimes impossible to keep the bait on the hook long enough to attract carp.

Small fish can be discouraged to some extent by using large, tough balls of paste, but more often than not, their persistence is such that even these are of little avail. Big night crawlers too, are often tweaked and whittled away by small and unwanted fish, such as bullheads. A carp usually takes a long time to make up its mind and very often there is no bait left for it to take.

One of the most popular baits is the so-called dough-ball. Flour and water paste balls are boiled until they become "dumplings". For a while, they survive the onslaughts of small fish, but in the end they succumb. Not so, however, the half-boiled potato.

In England, the half-boiled potato defeats the small fish every time. I have proved to my own satisfaction that it works in America too.

Potatoes, or potato portions about the size of a golf ball are fed into the area some time prior to fishing in order to commence the "education" process.

Carp eye any new bait with suspicion, but having sampled one or two portions with no ill effects, gain confidence and will eventually take the baited hook. Meanwhile, the potatoes will lie on the bottom, untouched by the smaller fish because they simply cannot whittle a potato down to takeable size.

Soaked corn is usually too tough for most small fish and where the carp are close at hand, is a good bait. When long casts have to be made, however, the addition of lead sinkers necessary for casting weight tends to reduce its efficiency. A carp will often take the corn, feel the resistance of the sinker (whether or not it happens to be of the slip type) and spit it out immediately.

Potatoes provide sufficient casting weight and can be used on a completely leadless tackle with a much better acceptance rate.

Where the bottom is of soft weed or mud, potatoes can be cut into thin slices so they sink with a swinging motion and come to rest lightly *on top* of the mud or weeds instead of becoming buried.

In many waters, and particularly in old and silted lakes, this is a special problem needing a special approach. The sliced potato deals with the soft bottom *and* the unwanted small fish, but where the latter do not exist, bread baits may be presented so as to rest lightly on or be suspended immediately above the soft bottom.

A balanced bait, made up of ordinary bread crust on the bend of the hook, weighted with

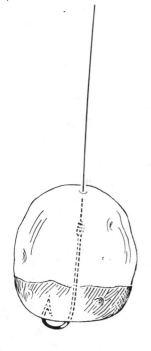

(Leave some skin on potato for casting aid)

Cut slice after hooking whole potato

just (and only just) enough paste on the shank to cause it to sink slowly, will come to rest and remain visible on the soft film of mud or weed without sinking into obscurity.

A cube of ordinary breadcrust anchored with a slip-sinker (the smaller the better) set an inch or two from the hook, depending on the depth of the weed or mud, is another practical solution to the problem. The natural buoyancy of the crust keeps it suspended just above the level of the mud or weed.

Where carp are active in the surface layer of warm water, it is reasonable to expect them to feed at some time or other in that layer. But it is of little use dangling a bait at the appropriate depth from a gaudy bobber. The presentation is entirely unnatural and carp are usually too smart to fall for stationary, suspended baits.

Carp will, however, often take baits that sink slowly under their own weight. It is well worthwhile contriving to make the bait sink *slowly* through the surface layer in the vicinity of a patrolling carp. Ordinary new breadcrumb can be made to do this very effectively by pinching the center portion tightly around the hook shank and leaving the outer edge soft.

Some experimentation is required to a- chieve perfection, but it is quickly mastered. Ideally the bread should float briefly while water is absorbed into the soft crumb and then sink very slowly as it becomes waterlogged. Carp will move long distances to intercept these baits.

Although it can be a tiresome way of fish- ing at times, it is by no means as tiresome as throwing lures for bass when there are no bass to be seen! Every move in the water can be noted, and with a degree of care, the bait can often be quietly dropped directly in the carp's line of vision.

Carp soon learn that discarded sandwiches and other oddments of floating bread are good to eat. Thus, I am surprised that more Ameri- can anglers do not fish for surface feeding carp with surface baits!

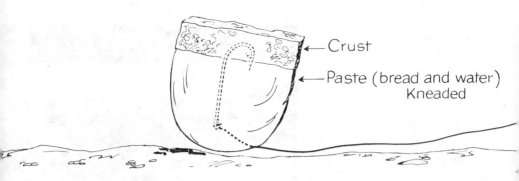

Crust

Paste (bread and water)
Kneaded

One of the most popular and widely-practiced types of fishing is surface lure angling for bass. It's exciting and spectacular as well as effective. But it is no more exciting, no more spectacular and certainly no more effective than surface bait fishing for carp. That is the most suspenseful and nerve-wracking kind of fishing I have ever practiced. Even today, after catching hundreds of carp that way, I still tremble with excitement as soon as the action starts.

The bait is a simple piece of bread crust into which a lightweight hook has been buried. Cast it so as to drift naturally. Let it come to rest against weed beds, bushes, boat dock piles or even the sloping bank itself. These are the spots where discarded food ends up naturally, and obviously where carp expect the pickings to be. If the hook bait is accompanied by several loose offerings, which follow the same line of drift, chances are probably increased. Loose pieces should be used sparingly, however. It is frustrating to see the loose pieces taken while the hook bait remains untouched! And it happens often enough.

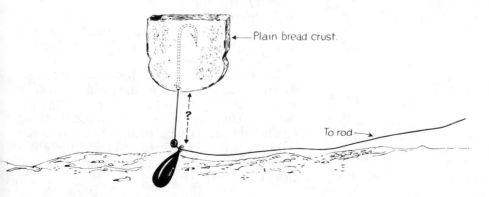

Plain bread crust.

?

To rod →

*For young and old . . .
Catchin' carp is an English
countryside pastime.*

A carp will sometimes swim up to a piece of floating bread, eye it, nose it, back off, return, swim around it and them leave it alone for half an hour. Then it may give it a mighty slap with its tail and eat the portions as they break up in the water.

Every so often, however, the big pair of lips will open and with a noise like water going down a bath plug, the floating bread will be sucked in like so much porridge! The temptation is to try and set the hook immediately, but it's not advisable to do so.

WAIT for the line to run off (and it almost invariably will) before striking. Then stand by for action! Carp hooked on the surface move off at a rate of speed that has to be seen to be believed!

After darkness, carp in lakes that are heavily fished or disturbed by day, will commence what is referred to in England as the "margin patrol". They are on the lookout for anything edible and are not particular. Floating bread is by far the best bait to offer and there is a special way of fishing this, known as margin fishing.

A rod rest is placed so that the tip of the rod hangs over the edge of water. If possible, the chosen spot should be one towards which the wind, if any, is blowing —— for obvious reasons. A strong, sharp hook is tied directly to the reel line. A piece of bread curst about half the size of a half-dollar is impaled and lowered onto the water, crumb side downwards, so that it hangs below the rod point and literally laps the bank. No line is allowed to touch the water, but some slack is drawn off the reel and left to lie on the bank. A loaf of bread, soaked and mashed into a thin gruel, can be poured onto the water as an attractor.

The hook bait may be taken with a great deal of noise on the carp's part or, strangely at night, very quietly and with no preliminaries. It is essential to have that slack line in readiness to allow the hook to be sucked in along with the bait. If the line is kept taut, the soft bread is often sucked off the hook.

In suitable conditions, margin fishing is one of the most deadly and certainly among the most exciting ways of catching big carp. Everything happens at close quarters and it is amazing how a big carp will manage to flop its way across water only a few inches deep to reach the margin crust.

Perfect quiet is essential, of course. It is important to remain out of sight, so the night hours are best for margin fishing. It can be practiced, however, from cover during the day on waters that are quiet and undisturbed by boats and human.

It is a way of fishing that has a great effect on the mind, often raising one to a fever-pitch of excitement that leads to failure because of violent or premature strikes or inattention to important details.

And when a great carp, hooked literally inches from the rod tip, decides to make for the other side of the lake like a runaway freight train in the darkness, a cold and calculating brain is required to handle the situation. If you have heart condition, don't try it. I mean it!

Throughout these ramblings I have insisted that, whenever possible, it is advisable to avoid leads, sinkers and bobbers. I stand by what I have written. It only requires a rod, line, hook and bait to catch a carp. Any additions to the tackle are entirely superfluous as long as the bait can be presented and bites registered effectively without them.

Circumstances sometimes alter cases, however, and there are odd situations which call for refinements in tackle and presentation.

Many carp are found in confined and fairly shallow areas. They live in thick, aquatic weeds and often the only fishable spots are small, clear holes no more than a few feet across. In these circumstances, it is almost impossible to let a fish run off with a bait.

Bearing in mind the carp's remarkable sensitivity to any kind of rod resistance, and the speed at which it can eject a bait upon feeling that resistance, (not *always* the case with unsophisticated American carp but I have encountered the problem from time to time) "instant strike" tactics are called for. This in turn calls for a very sensitive form of bite registration.

There are many techniques but drawbacks in almost every case. These must be consid-

Cork bobbin attached to rod rest.

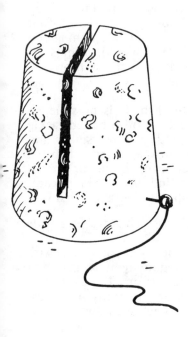

ered in regard to each particular situation. What is required is a bite indication which comes into effect the instant the bait is in the carp's mouth —— and that isn't always easy to arrange.

The line can be looped over the index finger or held lightly between thumb and forefinger of the left hand so that every tweak and pluck is felt immediately. This is fun when bites are frequent, but quite tiresome when they're not! It becomes difficult after a time to keep contact with the bait, the rod wavers and method becomes generally ineffective.

"Bobbin" or "dolly" type indicators are generally reliable where bites are bold and decisive. The rod is left in a rest (two rests preferably set so the rod is angled downwards towards the water) and a piece of dough, mud or even a fold of silver foil is pinched on to the line between the first two butt rings. A bite is registered immediately by a rising or falling of the "bobbin".

A split cork makes a good lightweight bobbin which can be attached permanently to the front rod rest by a length of cord or nylon. It comes off the reel when the strike is made but is always at hand for the next cast.

Probably the best method of bite detection incorporates the use of a slim float or small pencil bobber. An inverted bird quill stripped of its feather will do. So will a thin strip of reed or balsawood as long as it remains buoyant and does not become waterlogged.

Attach the float to the line with a wide, tight-fitting, rubber band at the bottom only. Next, place a large shot very near the hook. The tackle is set slightly deeper than the water (this method is obviously impractical in waters much deeper than 10 feet) and after casting, all is drawn taut until the bobber stands up clear of the water (see page 32).

When a carp sucks in the bait, the shot lying on the bottom is moved, the float *rises* in the water and keels over to lie flat on the surface.

Note that the bobber does *not* go under. Its effect, if anything, is to reduce resistance likely to be felt by the fish. Once it is seen lying flat, it may be reasonably assumed the bait is in the fish's mouth.

Picking up the rod and setting the hook should be done simultaneously, in one swift movement. Though it takes some practice, it is very effective.

The short American spinning or baitcasting rod is of little use for this kind of fishing. A rod of at least nine feet is essential to pick up the line and set the hook. I have used a 9-foot American Coho salmon rod (a spinning rod made from a soft fly rod blank) on most of my visits and found it perfect for nearly all my carp fishing.

River carp require different angling techniques than stillwater fish. It is possible, at times, to catch river carp on a baited tackle that has been cast with a heavy sinker and left to fend for itself in the current. If such a tackle is left long enough, sooner or later a carp is almost sure to find the bait. More carp, however, will undoubtedly be taken on a well balanced roving tackle which searches a wide area slowly.

Loading of the tackle is critical; fishing with it is easy. the only requirement is a rig that will settle lightly in the stream. It must not be so heavy that it will anchor fimly, nor must it be so light that it is whisked away by the current. It should barely hold bottom, in fact, and when cast, should bump slowly across and eventually settle downstream under the near bank. If it rolls across and down too quickly, it is too light; if it anchors midstream, it is too heavy and adjustments must be made.

A link-sinker made up of a fold of nylon monofilament and a given number of big split shots makes a simple and readily-adjustable slip sinker which can effectively deal with the situation.

Once the tackle is cast it begins its search. With rod held slightly high and line looped over the index finger, it is easy to detect bites — even from small fish. It's an active and very deadly way of catching carp in the right conditions.

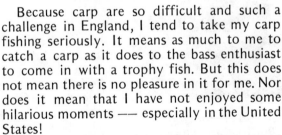

15

THE MAGIC OF CARP FISHING

Because carp are so difficult and such a challenge in England, I tend to take my carp fishing seriously. It means as much to me to catch a carp as it does to the bass enthusiast to come in with a trophy fish. But this does not mean there is no pleasure in it for me. Nor does it mean that I have not enjoyed some hilarious moments —— especially in the United States!

I have fallen in a lake with excitement; I have trod on my rod and smashed it. I have on one memorable occasion, hooked, played and landed a ten-pound carp in my underwear with the temperature below freezing and an inch of snow under my bare feet! I confess that I was fishing from the warmth and shelter of a moored houseboat at the time and thought I stood about as much chance of a carp biting as I did of getting a good cup of tea in America!

I caught a carp to order once too. Dan Gapen asked me to catch a carp for a photograph and informed me he would return at noon for the picture. He came back on time and at precisely that moment, a 13-pound carp decided to gobble my piece of bread. The only trouble being, I was in a restaurant at the time having coffee! I made it in time for the photograph, but I'll never really live that one down!

It's perhaps a good thing that carp fishing is generally looked upon as a light-hearted affair in America. I'd hate to think what the British Carp Study Group would think of that little episode! Those fellow *really* take their carp fishing seriously. Their records and reports are really worth reading by anyone who thinks there's nothing to carp catching.

I can recall times when I have been utterly depressed and despondent because of a scarcity of good fish. At such times, I have had half a mind to give it up altogether. But each time my morale has been lifted (and probably my sanity saved) by the capture of a hefty fish, the pleasure of netting a large fish for a close friend or by some small humorous incdent.

I've fished on and off for six years with a great American guy called Bill Hughes. In all that time, he's never allowed me to forget that I'm a bait fisher; a lousy Limey carp fisher not really smart enough to fish with lures and flies! He would never, he informed me, stoop so low as to fish for carp and I believed him. I might add that I ignored him also!

I believed him, that is, until the day he sat beside me and watched me catch five carp in the 10-14 pound class on a soft actioned rod and six-pound test line. He could stand it no longer.

He handed me a rod and instructed me to "tie on one of those hooks, pinch on one of those shots. Show me how to put that bread on".

And finally, handing me the baited outfit, he told me to "cast that bait out for me —— right there —— I'm gonna catch me one of them babies!"

Bill was hooked and later so was a 15-pound carp (bigger than I'd caught myself)! We ended

A devoted member of the British Carp Study Group admires a lunker "King" — name affectionately given to the Common Carp by English anglers.

the afternoon with, I believe, 13 carp and a gallery of interested onlookers. It was all very light hearted, as indeed nearly all American carp fishing tends to be, but there is scope I'm sure, for serious study of the species in the many waters available to the American angler.

I have already stated that I take my carp fishing seriously but that only means that I have an attitude towards carp —— an affection almost —— that is different from that of the American fisherman.

As I write this, I can see two trophy Northern Pike on my study wall. One weighs over 28 pounds, the other 32 pounds.

I catch, I suppose, a hundred or more northern pike per season. I have taken several 20-pounders, but I cannot look upon northern pike fishing as being anything more than a light-hearted affair. For in England, we look upon pike in much the same way as the average American looks upon carp —— fish that could well be done without!

Many Americans would be delighted to catch pike in the teens of pounds and I think they might well be persuaded to fish hard for them. I am prepared to fish hard for carp for the same reason.

There are still not enough carp in England to go around. I remember days when there were even fewer. There was something magic about carp fishing then, and although we caught smaller fish, we were, to some extent, responsible for the enthusiasm of today's happy, but serious, band of carp fishers. We passed the atmosphere on and others became involved in the magic and mystery of carp fishing. I would like to think that somewhere in America, too, there are men who can respect the carp for its fighting qualities and great heart.

Perhaps my affection for carp could be more readily understood —— if it was known to *what lengths* I have been prepared to go to —— and *what discomforts* I have been prepared to accept to come to terms with a big one.

I have caught plenty of big carp but none has given me more satisfaction than my first double-figure fish.

There came a time, somewhere around 1954, when I was invited to join the exclusive Carp Catchers Club. One of the necessary qualificaions for membership, however, was proof of having caught a ten pounder. I had to admit I was ineligible.

I was given one season to put matters right. Unfortunately, I was dogged by bad luck from the start. Conditions were bad at the beginning of the season. I despaired of ever achieving my goal, though I now had access to Woldale Lake which, at that time, was producing several double figure fish a season.

I felt there was a jinx on me. Things went wrong and frankly, I was heartily sick and tired of getting soaked to the skin, losing sleep and getting home an exhausted wreck.

It was in August that Dick Walker, my brother Ken and I traveled to Woldale Lake. As usual, it was raining hard. After erecting tents in the darkness we were faced with a decision. To fish, or to sleep and wait until the dawn. Ken and Dick decided to stick it out. I had with me a small one-man tent which I pitched close to shore. Then I set up the tackle and baited with a small boiled potato.

I sat hunched up in my small tent, miserable, wet and disconsolate. I wanted dawn to come. I wanted to go home. I'd had enough. I tried to doze and couldn't. I was too cold.

Then, just as the night was turning into day, my rod jumped in the rest and I grabbed the butt. The line was stripping off the open spool and I closed the bale arm and struck.

There was a crash above my head as the rod hit the branches of an overhanging tree which I'd forgotten about in my excitement. I felt a strange slackness in the line, cursed and struck again.

I was sure I'd lost my chance, but by a miracle the rod bent over to a solid resistance.

I stood up and began to control the fish which was running towards the middle of the lake. It didn't *feel* big. Dick and Ken were now emerging from the big tent and Dick stood by with the landing net.

The fish suddenly surfaced. It was enormous! At least it was enormous to me. Remember, I had never seen a carp bigger than six pounds. Slowly I brought it towards the bank, Dick reached out and gently lifted the big net and enclosed it.

"Stop trembling, Fred," he said, "it's yours." And he lifted it ashore.

Stop trembling! He might as well have asked me to stop breathing. I sat down on the wet grass. It had stopped raining but my legs and feet were soaked. It was some time before I realized I'd played the fish in my socks. But I didn't feel the wet or cold. Here was real magic -- my first double figure carp. I felt I'd earned it.

The fish weighed 16¼ pounds —— over ten pounds bigger than any carp I had caught previously. I wanted to keep it forever, but I put it back carefully. With one long, last look, I watched it swim away.

That is just one example of what carp fishing means to me and to hundreds like me. It is what carp fishing is all about and what it *could* mean to so many Americans, if only they'd give it a whirl.

The United States carp record is a 55 pounder, 11 pounds more than the English record. The U.S. record carp was *not* the result of years of study, tackle design, scientific approach and genuine dedication to carp fishing as was the case with the British record. In fact, it was accidental!

I am not in any way belittling the American record or its captor. I am simply trying to point out how different our attitudes are, and the great lengths our earlier carp fishing pioneers went in order to achieve results. Richard Walker's British record carp was caught as a result of a campaign lasting many years. It was caught by intent, not by accident.

I have no real ambition to break records. I'd like to, of course, but I do not have the necessary dedication even to try. I have fished the Willow Pitch with my bait in the very spot from which the record came, but I've never expected it to be broken.

I have, however, re-lived Richard Walker's experiences many times as he and I have sat together at Redmire pool and talked the dark hours away. The magic of that kind of carp fishing will always be with me. And as I sit on the banks of a quiet bay or secluded cove on any one of the big lakes of Wisconsin, Michigan, Illinois, Arkansas, Oklahoma, Oregon, Indiana, Missouri and many other American states, that same old magic comes to the fore.

There will always be a soft spot in my heart for "Old Buglemouth" and I hope you'll find one for him too. He's worth it!

16

COOKING CARP...
Or Try It You'll Like It!

The reluctance of many Americans to fish carp no doubt stems from the carp's ignominious reputation for having oily, tasteless flesh.

The carp probably earned this reputation more out of sight than taste. People who have seen carp thriving in badly littered, polluted water probably reach the conclusion that "anything that can survive in that gunk, MUST taste horrible!" And, there may be some semblance of truth in this philosophy, especially where the hardy carp continues to thrive in waters that have been severely despoiled by oil or industrial chemicals.

But amazing as it may seem, the flesh of the carp is usually firm and flavorful. During the very hottest summer months, however, carp — like any species of game fish — may have a musty flavor and soft flesh. But even then, their food value remains, although palatability may be somewhat decreased.

Maybe the best suggestion at this point is "Don't knock it, 'till you've tried it!"

Carp require just a few preliminary treatments during cleaning and may be cooked in the same manner as the more popular varieties of game fish.

Carp may be either scaled or fleeced. In fleecing, insert your knife under the scales. The scales and the outer layer of skin can then be chipped off with short strokes of the knife, working forward from the tail. This technique is relatively easy and well-adapted for preparation of carp in the kitchen.

In readying a carp for baking, cut off the head and tail and around the base of the large fins. Grasp the rear part of the fin, give a sudden pull forward and the fin bones and fins will tear away. By removing the fins in this manner, many of the nuisance bones are eliminated. Next, slit the belly and remove the viscera.

To remove the backbone, cut off the head and tail and lay the fish on its side. Hold the knife horizontal and cut with the tip of the blade along both sides of the backbone. Rib bones may be removed in the same operation, or by a separate cut.

The fish should lay open in one piece. Rib bones not cut away with the backbone may be pulled out with pliers or removed with the knife. The weight of the fish prepared by this method is about two-thirds of the whole fish. The fish is now ready to be folded over a prepared stuffing. Sew the back or truss for baking.

Carp may also be easily filleted. With a sharp knife, cut down through the flesh just behind the head. Next, cut along the backbone but not through it, all the way to the tail. Lift off the entire side of the fish. (Some anglers prefer to leave the slice of meat attached to the tail — either way is acceptable).

Turn the fish over and loosed the fillet on the other side in the same manner. With the skin on the bottom, start at the tail with the blade flat on the edge of the table or board. Pull on the carcass and resist with the knife. The weight of fillets is about 40 percent of the weight of the whole fish.

If the carp has a soft texture and lacks satisfactory flavor, taste may be enhanced by covering the dressed fish or fillets with the following mixture:

1 cup salt	2 tablespoons vinegar
1 large onion, ground or finely minced	1 teaspoon black pepper
	1/8 teaspoon mace

Mix the ingredients thoroughly. Place fish in a deep dish, cover all surfaces with the mixture and let stand for one hour. Rinse the fish thoroughly, and discard the mixture. It is now ready for cooking.

For carp steaks, select a large carp and dress it as for baking. The steaks, about one-half inch thick, are cut crosswise from the fish. The weight of steaks is about 60 percent of that of the whole fish. Two pounds of dressed carp will make 6 portions.

POPULAR AMERICAN RECIPES

Pan-Fried Carp

2 lbs. carp, pan-dressed
2 teaspoons salt
½ cup milk

½ cup all-purpose flour
½ cup corn meal
3 tablespoons fat or drippings

Cut fish into portions for serving. Salt on both sides and let stand for about 10 minutes. Dip the pieces in milk, drain, and roll in the flour and corn meal mixture. Melt fat in skillet. When fat is hot but not smoking, fry fish for about 10 minutes on each side.

Fried Carp Fillets

2 lbs. carp fillets about ¼ inch thick
½ cup all-purpose flour
½ cup corn meal

2 teaspoons salt
¼ teaspoon pepper
3 tablespoons vegetable shortening,
    or drippings

Cut fillets in portions for serving. Roll in corn meal, flour, salt and pepper mixture. Melt fat in shallow frying pan and fry fillets on both sides about 20 minutes, or until done. Serve, garnished with lemon and parsley. Serves six.

Broiled Carp Steaks

2 lbs. carp steaks (½ inch thick)
3 tablespoons fat or drippings
1 teaspoon salt

¼ teaspoon pepper
Paprika

Wipe carp steaks with a damp cloth, and place on rack of broiler pan. Dot top of fish with fat, season with salt and pepper, and sprinkle with paprika. Place in pre-heated broiler, two inches from the heat and broil for about 15 minutes. Turn steaks over, dot other side of fish with fat, season with salt, pepper, and sprinkle with paprika. Continue broiling for another 15 minutes, or until done.

Special Broiled Carp Fillets

2 lbs. carp fillets
1 teaspoon salt

¼ teaspoon pepper
3 tablespoons mayonnaise

Lay fillets skin-side down in a shallow, greased broiler-pan. Sprinkle fish with salt and pepper, and spread tops of fillets with mayonnaise. Place in a pre-heated broiler and broil two inches from the heat for 10 minutes.

Steamed Carp with Tomato Sauce

3 lbs. carp, dressed for baking
2 teaspoons salt

¼ teaspoon pepper
1 cup water

Cut dressed fish into portions for serving. Season with salt and pepper, and place on a rack over water in a pan with a tight-fitting cover. Steam for 10 minutes. Serve hot with tomato sauce.

Tomato Sauce

2 cups stewed tomatoes
1 small onion chopped fine
1 teaspoon salt
¼ teaspoon pepper

2 tablespoons melted butter
   or fortified margarine
2 tablespoons all-purpose flour

Simmer tomatoes, onion, salt, and pepper together for 10 minutes. Add the tomato mixture slowly to the combined flour and melted butter. Cook until thick, stirring constantly.

Baked Stuffed Carp

3 lbs. carp, dressed for baking

Stuffing

4 cups bread crumbs
3 tablespoons onion, finely chopped
¾ cup celery, finely cut (or ½
   teaspoon celery salt)

4 slices bacon, salt pork, or fat

6 tablespoons melted butter or
   fortified margarine
¾ teaspoon salt
⅛ teaspoon pepper
1 teaspoon sage

Cook the celery and onion for a few minutes in the butter. Mix the other ingredients and add to butter-mixture.

Wipe dressed fish with damp cloth and salt lightly inside and out. Stuff with dressing and sew or tie with string to retain stuffing. Place in a pre-heated oven and bake at 375°F. for 1 hour.

Pickled Carp

3 pounds carp fillets
1 quart vinegar
1 quart water
⅓ cup salt
1 teaspoon ground white pepper

¼ cup granulated sugar, or white
   corn syrup
1 teaspoon of whole mixed spices
1 large onion, sliced
½ cup of celery, coarsely cut

Tie the whole mixed spices in a piece of white cloth. Combine all the above ingredients except the carp, let come to a boil, and simmer for 20 minutes. Cut carp fillets into strips 3 inches long and ½ inch wide, and add them to the above liquid. Simmer for 15 minutes and allow to cool in the pickling stock.

Carp sticks can be pickled so as to be suitable for serving as appetizers or as cold cuts.

French Fried Carp

Cut a carp into fillets. Dry well after washing. Next, immerse the fillets in beaten-up egg and roll in mixture of bread crumbs, salt and pepper and with a touch of garlic. Deep fry in oil until done to taste. We would recommend peanut oil for deep fat frying primarily because of its thicker body and extra "zing" it adds to your taste buds.

90

POPULAR ENGLISH RECIPES

Baked Carp

Fillet carp and score. Cut up into 4-inch portions and place in a well-buttered baking dish.

Make a sauce with 1 ounce of butter, 1 ounce of white flour, 1 pint of milk, ½ cup of chopped onions, ½ cup of finely chopped peppers (green), 1 tablespoon of tomato puree and 2 ounces of cheese. Make sauce by blending flour and butter over heat and allowing to cool. Boil milk and add slowly to butter and flour "roux" stirring continually. Bring back to boil. Add peppers, onions, cheese, and tomato puree.

Add a small tin of mushrooms and a liberal sprinkling of salt and pepper to carp in dish. Pour over the hot sauce and cook in hot oven for 20 minutes. Garnish with sliced cucumber and lemon. Serve with boiled rice and chopped shrimp.

Carp Rolls

Fillet carp and cut into thin slices.

Mince ½ pound of fat bacon and 2 large onions and mix together with 1 cup of breadcrumb and a pinch of thyme. Scoop out the middles of several large tomatoes and add to the mixture, leaving tomato halves intact.

Spread the carp slices with mixture and make into long rolls.

Place remainder of mixture into tomato halves and lay in buttered baking dish between the fish rolls. Sprinkle with pepper, salt and a little Worcestershire Sauce. Cover completely with bacon rashers and cook for half an hour in fairly hot oven. Remove bacon when crisp and continue cooking carp until tender. Serve with crisp bacon.

CARP AU GRATIN

Cut carp fillets into fingers.

Fry 3 large onions in butter until golden brown and stir in 1 ounce of wheat flour. Remove from heat. Stir in 1 pint full cream slowly and re-heat. Add a little grated nutmeg, a little chopped parsley, sage, thyme, pepper and salt and a little mustard. Pour over fish and cover with thick layer of grated cheese. Bake in hot oven for an hour and brown under grill if necessary.

Carp Cakes

Cook carp in a little salted water and flake off bones.

For each ½ lb. of fish add ¼ lb. of mashed potato, a tablespoonful of finely chopped onion and a pinch of sage, a teaspoonful of chopped parsley, 2 teaspoons of anchovy essence, 1 egg, ½ ounce of white cooking fat, salt and pepper.

Mix thoroughly and shape into rounds. Roll in flour and fry in hot shallow fat until brown. Serve with french fries.

A wary eye - an artificial lure

In pursuit of Ol' Puckerpuss - a family group

They call it a trap - but its fishy

Well-hooked

"Fish On"

"Up and over you go"

17

A SECRET ABOUT BAD TASTE

You've heard it . . . you've ween it! Those folks who wrinkle their noses or huff off trailing the words "trash fish!" as they depart. Yeah, there are plenty of those kind around. But, just let them sink their teeth into a fishburger at the local fast food place and their disgust turns to pleasure. In both instances, they are referring to our friend, Mr. Carp, even though they aren't aware of it in the latter case.

It's true . . . often fish sandwiches you purchase in a fast food restaurant are made from carp meat. Oh, they also use several salt water species, but there is one chain that sells 75% carp meat in their fish burgers.

If this be the case, why haven't the doubting Thomases been able to detect those carpburgers by their taste. Certainly any fish that looks so ugly and is hated so badly can not taste so good . . . can he? You would think not, but I, for one, have never been able to distinguish between carp and cod. Maybe the similarity in taste comes from the way professionals clean carp meat.

In response to that last question I have no answer. However, I do have an excellent way of cleaning carp that have been tainted by a watery environment of mud or oil. It is a method that will work well on any species. White bass, catfish, drum and bass all taste better after being processed this spec-

93

ial way . . . fish that inhabit shallow, muddy lakes and back-waters where taste tainting can occur. My method of cleaning will not only remove foul taste but will, at the same time, firm up the meat, making it more palatable. Using a carp, let us detail the process.

The catch is filleted as it would be if the angler was going to pan fry it. Rib bones are left in the fish carcass (boneless filleting) or cut out after the slabbed meat is removed from each side. Next a sharp knife cuts the skin away from both fillets, exposing the horizontal lifeline. Normally the lifeline is easily identified by its reddish color. See Diagram No. 1.

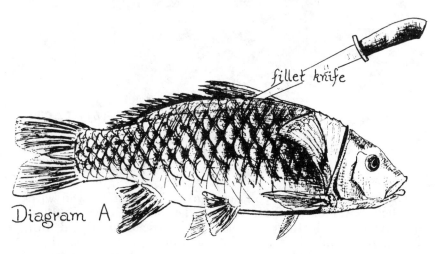

fillet knife

Diagram A

With both fillets facing skin side up (skin has now been re-moved), the angler takes an ordinary tablespoon and draws the cupped spoon bowl hard along the fillet's lifeline. Enough pres-sure must be exerted to see the red meat peel off the other-wise white meated fillet. Clean the entire length of lifeline off your fillet. See Diagram No. 2. Some folks will use a sharp knife to remove this red lifeline meat. That's fine. The main thing is to get rid of it. Often this section of a fish fillet holds the greatest amount of taste impurities.

Identification of the fish's lifeline is noted by looking at the fillet's central region and all along its outer skin side in a hori-zontal fashion. Here, halfway up the fillet's side, a thin sec-tion of dark red meat occurs. It can be as narrow as 3/4 inch or as wide as two inches. In all cases it runs the entire length of the fish's side, directly under the skin. It is the carp's sens-ing mechanism. Depth of the lifeline into a carp's meaty side can vary from 1/4 inch to nearly a full inch.

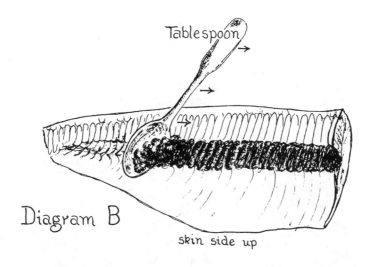

Tablespoon

Diagram B

skin side up

Step three is to cut up your fillets in chunk size pieces no more than three inches wide by fillet depth. A small fish will see five pieces of fish cut from one fillet while a large fish can have as many as a dozen.

Preparation of extra large carp fillets can be enhanced at this point of the process. Instead of three inch chunks, cut the larger fish's fillet in thin 3/4 inch slices. Due to wall thickness of these larger fish, thin slicing creates a piece of meat similar in size to that obtained from a five pound fish. Extra large carp fillets are carved from fish in the 20 pound and up category.

With the fish cleaned and cut up you now are ready for the final process that will see your carp meat firmed up and taste enlightened.

chunked pieces

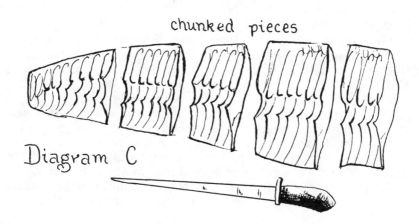

Diagram C

Leaving your chunked fish fillets to soak in fresh, cold water, and a solution of salt . . . cracked ice and cold water is prepared.

Take a large bowl, jug or pan which is capable of handling four times the amount of fish you've prepared. This extra room is needed for other ingredients that will be placed in the bowl.

Diagram D

First the bowl is half filled with crushed ice (small cubes will do, but I prefer cracked or crushed ice). To this ice, a full cup of salt is now added. This amount of salt is used when there is a minimum of a gallon of crushed ice used for base. A full cup of salt will vary with the amount of fish fillets to be processed. Five to eight pounds of meat is the measured amount used here. Pour salt directly over the ice.

Next, cold tap water is added in a similar amount to that of the ice. All three ingredients are mixed till salt has all but dissolved. Stirring gently for about two minutes should do it.

To this solution you now add the fish fillet chunks. Rotate ice, water, salt and meat till they are thoroughly mixed together.

Final action taken is to place this mixture of fish ice, and salt, bowl and all, in the refrigerator and allow it to sit overnight or at least 12 hours.

Prior to baking or pan frying, carp fillet chunks are removed, washed in fresh water and prepared in a normal manner.

As previously mentioned, a number of game fish that suffer from "bad taste" problems can have their reputations turned around by this remedy. White bass, in particular, can be upgraded and much to the amazement of many, become excellent table cuisine.

fat and full

SOFTCRAWS (Crawdad) WORK FOR TROPHY CARP

... Follow these instructions ...

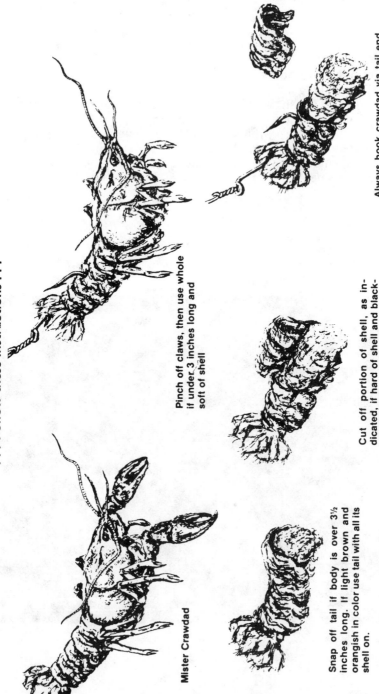

Mister Crawdad

Snap off tail if body is over 3½ inches long. If light brown and orangish in color use tail with all its shell on.

Cut off portion of shell, as indicated, if hard of shell and blackish/brown in color.

Pinch off claws, then use whole if under 3 inches long and soft of shell

Always hook crawdad via tail end (fan). Removal of shell allows scenting by hardshell crawdad.

There are times during the heat of summer when Carp prefer crawfish before any other food. With a similar taste to that of nightcrawlers this clawed critter will produce huge fish being that nightcrawlers are never found in lakes or rivers.

18

HOW TO CATCH BIG CARP

It was a hot, sultry day on Coon Wash backwaters. Heat waves danced erratically above algae-dotted surface waters. Occasionally a lazy bullfrog croaked his disgruntled response to the weight of such weather. These feeble attempts, once started, soon ended. Above, a searing hot sun forced rising surface vapors back down upon themselves. Such action created an oven roasting affect that caused man and beast alike to suffer. In the shade, a temperature gauge at Gil Tucker's boat livery showed 98 degrees.

Out over the main river bank, swallows from Branagan's Bluff swooped and flitted within inches of surface. The gnat and insect populations were taking a beating.

Gil Tucker had spent his entire life dispatching boats, bait and information along the Coon Wash backwater area. Heat and humidity were a way of life to old Gil, especially during the months of July and August. One hundred degree temperatures with 85% humidity weren't unusual. As a matter of fact, such weather was often best for catching Gil's two favorite fish . . . big carp and mudcats. Here, on the big river, huge fish were synonomous with hot weather.

I'd come to be at Gil's Boat Livery through a suggestion made by an old friend during a sports show in southwestern Illinois the previous winter.

Eddy hotspot

"If you can take heat and really want to catch a big carp, Dan, I'd suggest you mosey on down to Tucker's Bait Livery about the first week in August this coming summer," I'd been told.

"There just isn't anyone down along the big river bottoms who catches more or bigger carp than does Gil," my friend concluded.

Thus, I found myself in August, the fourth at mid day, standing on a broken board dock which penetrated deep into the eerie, dark surface of the Coon Wash backwaters. Walking the structure's length was a lesson in foot work and balance. Besides unsafe, rotten walk boards, there were those that had mysteriously disappeared completely. It was a challenge, to say the least.

"How bigga carp ya lookin' for, Dan?" came Gil's first question after I introduced myself and explained my reasons for coming.

"As big as I might land!"

"Well, ya better have a bit of heavy tackle, feller. This here carp along the backwaters 'er terrible big, ya know? That there stuff of yours don't look anywheres near strong enough!" he responded while looking dubiously over my selection of rods and reels.

Finally, after more verbal exchanges about line size and rod stiffness, Gil let it go, and we made plans to light out first thing after breakfast the next day.

100

"We're only goin' out near main channel. Be here about an hour before sunup," came my guide's last minute instructions.

With all arrangements made, I headed back to town , a hot/cold bath, and an afternoon nap. The drive from my home in Minnesota had been a tiring one.

As instructed, I stood on the dock, a pair of rods and reels and a tackle box in hand, exactly one hour after sunup. And . . . as programmed, old Gil was waiting, his ancient ten-horse Evinrude, chugging at idle, attached to a battered 15 foot jonboat.

"Ready, Dan? Got a bit of my special dough balls mix. Ya'll be amazed how goot it works!" came Gil's first response.

By his comment, I gathered that a special enticement would be used this day on Mr. Carp. I'd fished with dough balls before, but mostly for cats.

Diagram A

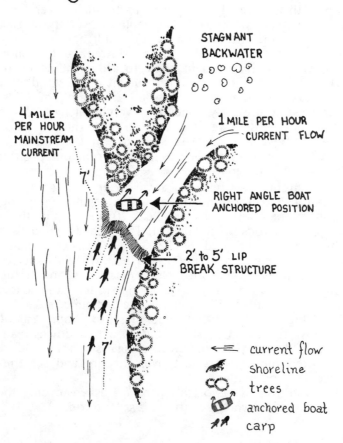

STAGNANT
BACKWATER

4 MILE
PER HOUR
MAINSTREAM
CURRENT

1 MILE PER HOUR
CURRENT FLOW

7'

RIGHT ANGLE BOAT
ANCHORED POSITION

2' to 5' LIP
BREAK STRUCTURE

7'

7'

current flow
shoreline
trees
anchored boat
carp

"Check to see if'n there's a hook anchor eye front, Dan. We'll need 'er down there where those big 'uns are found," Gil stated.

Sure enough . . . under the front seat a rusted hook anchor lie along with several yards of hemp rope. The same held true at Gil's end of the jonboat.

Gil placed a pair of heavy live bait rods and casting reel combos beside his faded bib overalls and thrust the old Evinrude in forward gear. Each of his rods reached over 7 1/2 feet in length. Around the Great Lakes these sticks were known as "Salmon Rods". Their butts were heavy, and their tips were fast . . . ideal live bait tools.

With surprising speed, Gil's tattered metal jonboat weaved its way through a series of black water side channels, eventually to emerge on a main river a mile down from Coon Wash. Overhead, a mat of woven cottonwood and river ash slid past, exposing the burning hot sun.

"We'll go up river a bit, a half mile more, and pole up to a place where the river run slides over a side lip. Big carp like ta work that water flow comin' in to main river from them stagnant washes, ya know," Gil shouted over the engine's roar as he headed upriver through a burst of sunlight.

A few minutes later the motor slowed, and anchors were tossed. We rested at a right angle to a descending lip of water which entered the main river through a tall stand of cottonwood. (See Diagram A for an understanding of Gil's secret big carp structure). By placing a varying length of rope on the twin anchor set, we were able to cock the jon to one side. This would give both anglers an equal shot at the carp which now rested downstream, below the lip, from our position. (See boat position in Diagram A)

I had brought with me a large, open face spinning outfit, one best suited for large pike and a regular rig loaded with 10 pound line. Both Gil's rigs held 20 pound plus line weight. Gil rigged his rods with large, 1 1/2 inch dough balls brought forth from an old lard bucket. They had been hand rolled prior to our departure. Later I was to learn Gil's special dough balls were inner rigged with No. 1/0 short shank treble hooks inside. I would use my regular rig which was loaded with crawlers and a Bait-Walker sinker in the one ounce size.

"The big 'uns don't hold too close to shore. Ya'll find'em just below the lip and strung out in a row downstream about 50 feet off shore," Gil commented as he cast his first rod.

I spotted the crawlers just over the dip and set the rod in a convenient rod holder.

"Gil, can you use two rods here?" I asked, eyeing the stoop shouldered angler who now lifted his second rod.

A Creek enters

"Don't know . . . why not?" came an unexpected, gruff answer.

So much for that question. If he wasn't worried, I sure wasn't going to question his tactics. But, just to be safe, I fished with one rod.

Gil went on to explain why he always found large carp in this spot. It seems the water coming out of the stagnant backwater area was a couple degrees warmer than the mainstream currents. This not only helped draw huge fish, but also provided a flow of food coming into the main river. He claimed that big carp found the natural lip drop an enticement . . . something to do with aeration of the water flow in hot weather.

Gil added that large insect larvae, reared in the backwater's muddy, black bottom, were known to work their way out across the lip. Big carp loved juicy stonefly and other large larva, according to Gil.

Water depth in which Gil's targeted carp staged ran from seven to ten feet along an old backwater channel bed. (Refer to Diagram A)

My rod jumped first, and before long a small, four pound carp came to net.

"Ya won't see me catching that size, fella, " commented my guide with a smile.

My answer had something to do with me being from Missouri, and I, too, grinned a sheepish smile.

Gil had used a 1 1/2 oz. egg sinker held 30 inches up his line via a match stick stop. Presentation was directly on bottom, downstream from the lip structure.

It was another five minutes before Gil's first rod triggered a "tap-tap" indicating fish. Gil gently removed the rod butt from its holder, lowered the rod tip, then thrust hard backwards. He was solidly hooked to a submerged freight train. Whatever it was, Gil's big ol' rod bent double, and his star drag reel squealed as line peeled off. Fifteen minutes after it began, with a second outfit peeling line from its rod holder, Gil brought a 26 pounder to boat. Quickly he was released, and the fight to secure fish two began. This one proved to be slightly smaller, 21 1/2 pounds.

About the time that the 21 pounder came to net I managed to hook and land a seven pounder . . . big deal!

Gil claimed that size of his dough ball had a lot to do with the size of fish he was taking. I'd heard the same thing from an Englishman friend of mine. Too small a bait caught only too small carp. Make the bait to fit the size of the fish's mouth . . . that was Gil's theory.

It later became evident that Gil's dough ball recipe had something to do with his success. Texture and feel of the dough balls was smooth, slippery and natural feeling. Later I learned my guide's secret recipe consisted of the following:

Ingredients:

2 cups of corn meal
2 cups of water
1/2 cup of syrup (corn or Karo)
1 tablespoon anise oil
4 tablespoons of vanilla extract

Gil explained that all the items in his dough ball recipe were easily available in your local store. The anise oil will be found in a drug store. Next, stir all these ingredients in a pot over a low fire until they come to a boil. Stir constantly after they've boiled and allow to simmer for about eight minutes. Allow to sit and cool for about 25 minutes.

Next, flour a baking pan and roll your mixture into small balls the size desired. The bait can either be kept in balls or under cover in a container in its finished form.

Gil added one last touch to the dough balls. Once rolled into the desired size, they were like most other dough balls, dipped in a secret solution. I was told it contained the bile ducts of catfish, soft honey, carp blood and more vanilla extract. I cannot confirm this, but the watery solution did have a dark red appearance.

I believe the dough ball recipe Gil used is rather common among carp fishermen, but it must have been that reddish solution that helped make his secret dough balls work so well. In testing at later dates, I found it to work both ways but must admit that when dipped in the final solution, they did produce more fish . . . or so it seems.

One thing must be noted. Gil's 1 1/2 inch dough balls did catch bigger carp than those I'd used over the years. Mine had always been under an inch in diameter.

Below the channel lip where intruding backwater waters entered mainstream, we took three more large carp. One tipped scales at 17 1/2 pounds, another at 27 even, and a final monster at 32 pounds. Gil took all the big fish except the 17 1/2 pounder. I managed this fish after losing three which seemed much larger. And, I managed only to hang these fish after switching my bait for Gil's favorite recipe.

By referring to Diagram B, you'll note the construction of Gil's dough ball and how a treble hook is implanted in some. Shown also are the two methods of weighted sinkers we used to hold bait on bottom below the lip. In each case a 24 to 30 inch dropback line stretches out beyond the sinker to which the treble hook is tied. In my case, I used a 2/0 short shank single hook around which the dough ball was fixed.

Diagram B

"GILS" 1½ inch
doughball

My day with Gil Tucker didn't end at the lip hole. Two hours after arriving we headed upstream once again. This time we'd fish a large river eddy structure where a "flood cut" emptied and another area just behind a river island.

Like so many other slow circulating big river pools, the one Gil selected was better than two blocks in length. It consisted of large twin eddies which rested along the river's western (left) bank. The structure was housed by a shoreline protrusion along its downstream side. Within this slow-turning eco system I soon discovered big carp swam. Refer to Diagram C to better explain the following information.

To properly "straight line" the dough balls down on the carp at point No. 2 on Diagram C, we anchored our jonboat at a similar angle to that done in Diagram A. (Straight lining is a method of presenting your bait directly downstream from rod holding position.) Bait offerings were cast directly in front of incoming water from the flood cut where the structures eddies converged. Our first presentations were made at a point half way between the boat and the point marked No. 2. Second presentation was made right on point No. 2. Both produced large carp plus a few smaller ones.

Our second anchoring positioning on the structure in Diagram C was downstream from the river island but upstream from the point marked No. 1. Here, boat anchorage held between influxing currents created by the small island stream and circulating eddy wash. Bait positioning once again would be straight lined downstream from the boat along the current cut between main eddy and the island eddy.

Although some big carp positioned directly downstream from the island at point No. 1, many others held along the current cut along the main eddy's outer edge. Once again, Gil used his special dough balls to entice the big fish, and once again my crawlers failed to entice anything but small fish. We fished in water that varied from five to eight feet in depth with a sandy gravel bottom. This fact matched with comparable bottom texture that held large carp on the upper Mississippi where I lived. Small rock sand and gravel bottom combined with slow moving water seemed always to house large fish. Silt, black bottom, mud or fine sand produced small fish or no fish at all. Another fact held true! Larger carp seemed to hold along the outer eddy areas or current cuts of circulating water structure. And, not one of our large fish had been caught on water under four feet. Only fish on the two to ten pound range were seen or caught in such shallow water.

There will be times when large carp work shallow waters, but the rule of thumb best followed is that water structure over four feet, six to eight preferable.

Gil and I worked throughout the heat of that day. It was nearly four in the afternoon before we bumped alongside his battered dock.

"Well, whadaya think Gapen? Did we git the big 'uns or not?" my guide questioned.

He was right. We'd taken a lot of big carp, more than I'd ever seen taken in one day ever. And, more than I knew could be taken from one area by two anglers in a day, a week, or a month!

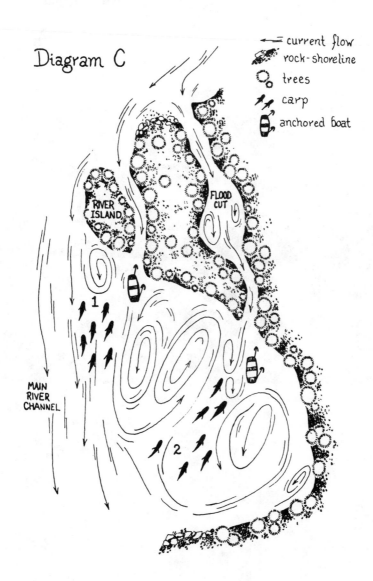

I learned much that day. One thing was that if you're going to handle large carp, do it with the proper equipment. Next time my salmon rods would go along.

And . . . if credit was to be given to any one reason Gil and I had taken nine fish over twenty and two over thirty, it would have to go to Gil's special dough ball recipe. Yup, that must have been it.

Well . . . maybe the heat had something to do with it?

Or . . . maybe that Ol' River Rat just knew a hell of a lot more about Old Puckerpuss than I.

Success at last . . . A huge carp is netted

the Elk

19

OL' PUCKERPUSS

And so . . . we've written a book on Mr. Puckerpuss, the some-times hated, sometimes loved, sometimes worshipped and often despised fish who swims within most waterways throughout our world. Our writing has taken you across America and onto the continent of Europe from whence he came. We even referred to the Carp's ancient birthplace, Mother China. It has been learned that everywhere but here in America, Mr. Carp is treasured for fighting, food and historical characteristics. However, for reasons never really established, America's greeting to the mention of 'carp' has always been a distaining turn of the head or a repulsive barrage of words. Why is this? Why has America's attitude towards old puckerpuss been so distorted? Why do anglers in America hate Ol' Puckerpuss?

Could it be this heavy scaled ugly fish is disliked because he adapts to the worst of polluted conditions manufactured by man? Is he maligned because he survives where other die? Is it taste? That can't be so, for carp are treasured dearly for their high rate of protein in both Europe and Asia. Certainly, it cannot be this fishes ability to fight his would-be aggressor. Pound for pound, there are few who equal his strength while fighting. Carp may well be considered the 'bulldog' of our freshwater fishery. Though he may not dance acrobatically across water surface, his deep stubborn, long running fight is the match for any angler.

If none of these, then why? Could it be that American anglers have placed an unfair label of "trashfish" upon Ol' Puckerpuss? I think this is so!

Let's examine the average response of most American sportsmen upon viewing a carp recently caught by a fellow angler or one of their children. Most will laugh disgustedly, an action which immediately sets forth a negative air upon the scene. First words probably will involve "trash fish" or "smelly thing" or "bury-it-in-the-garden" or "for gods sake . . . you aren't going to keep that are you?"

If it's a child who holds a 'just-caught' carp, the observing adults will be a little kinder, but the end result will remain the same.

Such putdowns of this imported fish began almost immediately after the first German carp swam our eastern waters. He had been brought to America to provide a manageable resource which would easily be farmed. But, like so many other well intentioned actions this one went astray. Carp somehow got into the eastern waters of the America's trout, then a favorite of the high minded American sportsman. Once dispersed there was no stopping Mr. Carp, he slowly and stubbornly crept his way across the continent, one waterway to another. Like the wolf, this finny species from Europe became a villian for all to despise. If America's fishery had a problem, it naturally was blamed on Ol' Puckerpuss. Get rid of the carp and you'd rid yourself of the problem. Today this thinking still exists in many segments of our fishing community.

But, riding ourselves of Mr. Carp may not be the only answer or solution to our fishery problems. Today we must combat other problems such as pollution, habitate loss, food base change, specie inbalance and natural environmental change. The carp is here to stay! He will not go away and in most structures where he now exists, carp have found their place.

If Mr. Carp can find his place then, it seems only natural that we American anglers put aside our prejudices and begin to utilize the sport and fun which can be had in pursuit of Ol' Puckerpuss. Let it begin this year.

With my book all but done, there must be a few things I failed to pen or I left unsaid.

Did you know that carp readily rise to the fly when proper conditions exist along certain river systems. Mayfly hatches are seen to draw carp to surface along eddy pools where dieing insects compress along converging current cuts. Properly presented dry flys readily enhance carp into striking.

110

Along the upper Mississippi River corridor, where the shallow rocky riverbed leaves little room for weed growth, Carp are seen to eagerly hunt and chase down small crawfish in rocky ripples. It is here that a crawdad colored, short billed crankbait causes carp to strike a lure.

It's a well known fact that waters throughout the nations central region see carp taken on small yellow jigs presented in a slow manner. It may amaze some that such jigs (1/32 & 1/16 oz.) are not tipped with any type of livebait for added enticement. The yellow jigs are fished just as they come from the store bought package.

All over the nation, carp readily become victim to a small 1/8th oz. Ugly Bug Jig in brown color when tipped with a small piece of nightcrawler. The crawler tipping should measure no more than one inch. The lures rubber legs and brown colors represent that of a hellgrammite or insect, favorite food base for carp, while the scent from a crawler is added enticement to cause the strike.

In many areas carp have been taken on minnows. Wherever this occurs, there is another happening which occurs. Small nickel plated jigging spoons often take carp. Possibly the flashing nickel jig reminds the carp of an injured minnow as it is jigged along the bottom.

Corn, nightcrawlers, crawdads, hellgrammites, garden worms, potatoes, dough balls and even marshmellows will take carp, but it is those special dough and cornmeal recipes which really take carp. Use single, double or treble hooks. Sinkers can be split shot, egg sinkers, pinch-on lead, three-way rigs or bait-walker sinker rigs to present such bait.

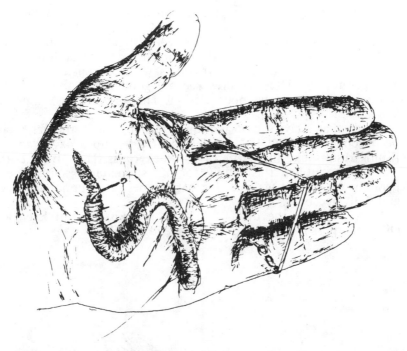

One thing for sure . . . 99% of your carp will be taken by working lake or river bottom. Carp are definitely a bottom feeder. Because bottom texture has a bearing on how well carp are able to detect your offering, it is advisable to work bottoms which are not soft or silty . . . look for sand or gravel or even rock.

When working a water system where other species are present, it is a noticable trait of carp to head for shallow water once your hook is set. This "running for shore" tendency can be an easily identifiable way of guessing what you have on the line. Once the hook is set, the quarry heads directly at shore in a right angle to the current. As shoreline nears, carp will continue up to shore edge as long as there is enough water to swim in. Then your hooked fish will abruptly head upstream, racing as close to shoreline as possible. Twenty feet into this run, he will reverse direction and head on back downstream. Next, another run out into main current is made, generally done at right angle to current flow once again.

In a lake a similar technique is enacted by a hooked carp with the angle towards shore varying according to the amount of pressure placed upon the fish by the fisherman.

If roots or weeds are easily available along the shoreline, you may well see your fish race beneath each and every one of them in a maneuver which appears rather clever. In many cases, along river channels, I have lost huge carp which suddenly found current exposed tree roots an easy escape. Knowing such hinderance exists might see the angler load his reel with heavier stronger line.

As this book began, I must end it with a note of fun. Dave Conn, my very dear fishing friend, saw fit to mistakenly kiss a carp one day. Thus we now see my good friend and his huge finny friend gracing this book's cover. The lesson being . . . never kiss a carp!

Other than Dave's one and only misjudgement the carp has been good to he and I. No fish can brighten up a day of poor fishing results like the battle of Ol' Puckerpuss. Though we both may fail to utilize this fellow for our shorelunch, waiting desperately for a wily walleye, his battle doesn't go unnoticed and gratefully accepted.

Oh . . . what the devil . . . why not kiss a carp! Even an Ol' Puckerpuss needs a bit of love once in a while.

*Relax . . . Sunshine . . . Cool breezes
and a backwater where Ol' Puckerpuss
is found to lazily roam.*

FISH CATCH and RELEASE CHARTING RECORD

No matter what fish comes to hand . . . no matter how it was caught . . . no matter where it was caught, an angler should chart and record those fish worthy of being called a trophy. Thus it is these final pages of my carp book that are set aside for such records. Knowledge retained in these records can enhance the fisherman's future angling success when referred to prior to setting forth. Where a large game fish held last summer may see an equally large companion fish taking up feeding station on structure. If this large fish took a shelled crawdad tail two years ago on this structure, on this date, his replacement may also want an identical enticement today.

Thus it is that I suggest every angler chart his "big" fish so that success in future outings will once again be his.

Good fishing,
Dan D. Gapen Sr.

DATE	FISH	TIME	LURE OR BAIT	LOCATION & STRUCTURE	LINE	PRESENTATION & WATER CONDITION

116

DATE	FISH	TIME	LURE OR BAIT	LOCATION & STRUCTURE	LINE	PRESENTATION & WATER CONDITION

DATE	FISH	TIME	LURE OR BAIT	LOCATION & STRUCTURE	LINE	PRESENTATION & WATER CONDITION

DATE	FISH	TIME	LURE OR BAIT	LOCATION & STRUCTURE	LINE	PRESENTATION & WATER CONDITION

DATE	FISH	TIME	LURE OR BAIT	LOCATION & STRUCTURE	LINE	PRESENTATION & WATER CONDITION

DATE	FISH	TIME	LURE OR BAIT	LOCATION & STRUCTURE	LINE	PRESENTATION & WATER CONDITION

DATE	FISH	TIME	LURE OR BAIT	LOCATION & STRUCTURE	LINE	PRESENTATION & WATER CONDITION